SPAGHETTI SAUCES

Authentic Italian Recipes from
Biba Caggiano

Photographs by Jessica Nicosia-Nadler

GIBBS SMITH
TO ENRICH AND INSPIRE HUMANKIND

First Edition
2 3 4 5   11 12 13 14 15

Text © 2011 Biba Caggiano
Photographs © 2011 Jessica Nicosia-Nadler

Published by
Gibbs Smith
P.O. Box 667
Layton, Utah 84041

1.800.835.4993 orders
www.gibbs-smith.com

Designed by Debra McQuiston
Printed and bound in Hong Kong

Gibbs Smith books are printed on paper produced from sustainable PEFC-certified forest/controlled wood source. Learn more at www.pefc.org.

Library of Congress Cataloging-in-Publication Data
Caggiano, Biba.
Authentic Italian recipes from Biba Caggiano / Biba Caggiano ; photographs by Jessica Nicosia-Nadler. — 1st ed.
      p. cm.
ISBN 978-1-4236-0688-8
1. Cooking (Pasta) 2. Tomato sauces. 3. Cooking, Italian. 4. Cookbooks. I. Title.

TX809.M17C326 2011
641.5945—dc22

2011003615

To my six grandchildren: Andrew, Alex, Aidan, William, Lucy, and Jack. To my two daughters: Carla and Paola, and their husbands, Tim and Brian. And to my husband Vincent, who is at his happiest when we are all at the dinner table together enjoying the food and the wine.

CONTENTS

4 Introduction

8 Cheese

30 Pesto

46 Quick Tomato

66 Vegetable

86 Seafood

106 Ragu

124 Acknowledgments

125 Index

INTRODUCTION

There is an old Italian saying, *A tavola non s'invecchia*—"at the table one never grows old." That is possibly why Italians used to spend a great deal of time around the table—savoring good food, sipping good wine, and enjoying their company.

Today, most women work outside of the home and the food they prepare daily is simpler than what the generation before them served. A plate of pasta might be followed only by a salad and cheese. The three-to-four-course dinner seems to be a thing of the past, or it is prepared only for special occasions.

This is a cookbook about spaghetti— a string pasta that most people in the world, young and old, love. Many of the sauces in this book are quick, inspired, and uncomplicated, with perhaps the exception of the ragu chapter, and are absolutely delicious. Just think that while the water comes to a boil and cooks the pasta, you can make a tasty sauce. How great would it be to come home from work and know that in 15 to 20 minutes you can have a wonderful pasta dish on the table?

SPAGHETTI, THE ITALIAN GOLD

I was born and raised in Bologna, a city well known for its amazing homemade pasta, and fed a daily diet of tagliatelle, tortellini, ravioli, and lasagna. Yet today, when I crave pasta, I often reach for a box of factory made spaghetti. Perhaps it is the immediacy of the product that is so appealing. No hassle, no fuss. Just reach for the box and drop the pasta into boiling water. Nothing can be quicker and appease hunger like a plate of perfectly cooked spaghetti.

For many people who have traveled to Italy, "spaghetti" conjures up images of a sunny land. A land of white beaches, tranquil seas, high mountains, magnificent cities, quaint towns, and gregarious people who are at their happiest when they gather around the table with a steaming bowl of wholesome, mouthwatering pasta.

Of the many types of regional Italian pasta, spaghetti is perhaps the most familiar, the least threatening, and the most immediate. Boisterous and colorful in the South, it is more restrained and luscious in the North. Throughout the centuries, people all over the world learned how to preserve grain against the vagaries of weather, molds, and insect infestation. They learned how to turn grain into flour and eventually into pasta with its innumerable shapes. Spaghetti, with its rich golden color, is Naples' contribution to the regional Italian table and, without any doubt, is the most popular pasta in the world and a symbol of all things Italian.

Spaghetti is also the perfect dish to prepare for an impromptu get together. *Ci facciamo una spaghettata*? —"How about a nice plate of spaghetti?" The *spaghettata* is an Italian ritual. It takes place in someone's home or in a homey trattoria. The only rule is that the spaghetti be tossed with quick, appetizing sauces and that it gets to the table while hot—and, of course, that it is enjoyed in a spirit of conviviality.

When I have family or friends over for a spaghettata, I use seasonal ingredients as well as ingredients I have in my well-stocked pantry. Canned Italian tomatoes, white tuna packed in oil, anchovies, olives, garlic, capers, sun-dried tomatoes, dried porcini mushrooms, roasted bell peppers, marinated artichoke hearts, and so on, can be used all year around. In spring and summer, I take advantage of what the season has to offer; ripe tomatoes, spring onions, fresh basil, peas, asparagus, and zucchini. I often enhance the flavor of the sauces with some diced prosciutto, smoked pancetta, or really great olive oil. And the nice thing is all of these sauces can be made in the time the water comes to the boil and cooks the pasta.

Because I work at my restaurant six days a week, on Sunday, when my grandchildren come over for dinner, this is the type of food I like to cook. Quick, stress free, flavorful sauces tossed with spaghetti. I look at my grandchildren's faces as they try to twirl the spaghetti around their forks and some strands fall back onto the plate in spite of their efforts . . . it is pure magic! Then a small voice says, "Nonna, more spaghetti pleeease!"

SPAGHETTI AND OTHER PASTA SHAPES

Spaghetti and other dry pastas are made with durum wheat flour and water. This dry pasta, which has the golden color of wheat, is made in factories all over Italy using a large mixer and extruded by putting the dough through different sizes of metal dies to form the various shapes. These shapes are then dried in temperature-controlled chambers.

In choosing factory made pasta, look for an imported Italian brand. Some of my favorites are: Rustichella d'Abruzzo, Del Verde, Martelli, Barilla, La Molisana, De Cecco, and Fini. Factory made Italian pasta, when properly cooked, swells considerably in size while maintaining its toothsomeness and immediacy. Just reach for a box of imported pasta and in no time at all you will have a mouthwatering pasta dish on your table. Spaghettini, linguine, vermicelli, rigatoni, and penne may be used instead of spaghetti to be served with your favorite sauces.

HOW TO COOK PERFECT SPAGHETTI

- Always use a large pot with plenty of water, about 6 quarts.
- When the water boils, add a few pinches of salt and the spaghetti.
- Cook, uncovered, stirring a few times. If there is plenty of water in the pot, the spaghetti will not stick together.

• The cooking time of spaghetti depends on its thickness and brand. Read the cooking instructions on the package, but taste the spaghetti for doneness a few times during cooking. Perfectly cooked spaghetti should be tender but still firm to the bite.
• Once the spaghetti is cooked, drain and toss it immediately with the sauce in a large warm bowl or in the skillet where the sauce is simmering.
• Never rinse the spaghetti, it will wash off the layers of starch that helps bind the sauce with the pasta.
• And finally, remember that pasta waits for no one—my mother's favorite motto. If pasta is made to wait, in the skillet with the sauce or in the dish, it will become overcooked and limp.

THE DRY PANTRY

The following are basic staples that should always be available in an Italian pantry. These ingredients can be kept for months and they are the key to the success of your dishes. Basic non-perishable items such as dried pasta, rice, canned tomatoes, dried mushrooms, olive oil, capers, and anchovies are some of my favorites, and they can be quickly transformed into a tasty sauce.

• Anchovies - packed in oil, are chopped and used for pasta sauces.
• Canned Plum Tomatoes - San Marzano peeled tomatoes are perhaps the best canned variety. They can easily be transformed into a quick delicious tomato sauce.
• Capers – another useful ingredient to keep in your pantry. They go very well with olive oil, olives, sun-dried tomatoes, and many other ingredients to make a caper sauce.
• Dried Herbs - when fresh herbs are not available, keep dried oregano, rosemary, sage, thyme, and marjoram at hand. Use them as soon as you can and in moderation. The older they are, the stronger their flavor is.
• Extra Virgin Olive Oil - an amazing ingredient to be added to most Italian dishes.
• Garlic - fresh only, to be minced and added to pasta sauces in moderation.
• Olives - green and black, great to chop and add to a pesto or pasta sauce.
• Other Dried Spices - such as cinnamon and nutmeg; use them as soon as you can.
• Pasta – spaghetti or linguine, ziti, bucatini, penne, rigatoni, and shells imported from Italy, just to mention a few.
• Pine Nuts - often added to pesto sauces.
• Porcini - wild Italian mushrooms that grow under chestnut trees. Dried porcini lasts several months and enriches a pasta sauce instantly.
• Sun-Dried Tomatoes - keep in your pantry to use when fresh tomatoes are out of season.
• Wine – (besides for drinking) is often used to give body and taste to a sauce. The better the wine, the better your sauce tastes.

THE REFRIGERATED PANTRY

Fresh ingredients look better and taste better when used within a few days. While the dry pantry ingredients can be kept for months, the ingredients in the refrigerator should be purchased and used while they are fresh. Just keep in mind that the secret of Italian cooking lies in its freshness and the fidelity to its ingredients.

• Butter – unsalted, is mild and delicious. A pat of sweet, unsalted butter added to a hot tomato sauce will tame the strong taste of the tomato.

CHEESES
• Gorgonzola - a typical cheese of Lombardy with a strong, yet creamy texture. It is great for sauces or served with wine-roasted pears.
• Mascarpone - is a soft, buttery, mild cow's milk cheese. It is used as a table cheese or as an ingredient for desserts.
• Mozzarella - a southern Italian cheese that is light and delicate. It is a perfect ingredient for pizza or served with fresh ripe tomatoes and basil.
• Parmigiano-Reggiano - is one of the best cheeses of Italy and is made in the flat land of Emilia-Romagna. Buy a nice chunk and use it grated over pasta, soup, risotto, or gnocchi. Parmigiano is not used over seafood because its fragrant aroma can overwhelm the delicate taste of fish.
• Pecorino Romano - one of the oldest Roman cheeses. It has a peppery taste that coats and lingers after it is grated over the pasta.
• Ricotta - is a soft, fresh cheese that can be used in myriad ways. It is great for the filling of homemade pasta and pastries.
• Taleggio - is a whole cow's milk cheese typical of the region of Lombardy in Northern Italy. It has a creamy, mild, and sweet flavor and can be used in cooking or served at the end of a meal with a crisp white wine.

MEATS
• Pancetta - this unsmoked Italian bacon is cured in salt and spices and aged for a few months. Pancetta is rolled up like a salami and its unique savory taste is essential to many Italian dishes.
• Prosciutto di Parma - is unsmoked, salted, and air-cured ham made from the hog's hind thigh. This magnificent ham can be eaten sliced as an appetizer or a snack, or diced as a component of many pasta sauces and pasta fillings.
• Speck - is smoked Italian ham from the Alpine mountains of Northern Italy. It can be eaten as an appetizer or diced as a component of many pasta sauces.

CHEESE

10 Butter, Cream, Parmigiano, and Nutmeg

11 Butter, Sage, Ricotta, and Parmigiano

12 Fresh Tomato Sauce with Ricotta Cheese and Basil

14 Fresh and Sun-Dried Tomatoes with Pecorino Cheese

15 Mozzarella, Cherry Tomatoes, and Basil Capri Style

16 Pancetta, Eggs, Parmigiano, and Mascarpone Cheese

17 Pancetta, Hot Pepper, Olive Oil, and Pecorino

18 Pancetta, Eggs, Peas, and Parmigiano

20 Prosciutto, Cream, and Swiss Cheese

21 Pecorino Romano Cheese, Pepper, and Crisp Garlic

22 Prosciutto, Butter, Sage, and Parmigiano

23 Smoked Mozzarella, Sun-dried Tomatoes, Capers, and Herbs

24 Smoked Pancetta, Hot Pepper, Saffron, and Pecorino Cheese

25 Taleggio, Cream, and Parmigiano

26 Uncooked Tomatoes, Mozzarella, and Basil Capri Style

28 Walnut-Gorgonzola Sauce

BUTTER, CREAM, PARMIGIANO, AND NUTMEG

CON BURRO, PANNA, PARMIGIANO E NOCE MOSCATA

This preparation is typical of many Italian regions. When I was a child, my mother prepared it for me, my sister, and my brother, but instead of spaghetti, she made these amazing tagliatelle (homemade noodles) that were simply wonderful topped with this easy sauce.

1 pound spaghetti

4 tablespoons unsalted butter

1½ cups heavy cream

⅓ teaspoon freshly grated nutmeg

Salt, to taste

1 cup freshly grated Parmigiano-Reggiano cheese, divided

1 Cook spaghetti in boiling salted water according to the package directions. When pasta is almost done, scoop up and reserve about ½ cup of the cooking water.

2 Meanwhile, heat the butter in a large skillet over medium heat. As soon as the butter begins to foam, add the cream and nutmeg and season with salt. Simmer until the cream just begins to thicken, 2 to 3 minutes. Turn off the heat under the skillet.

3 Drain pasta, leaving just a little water attached to its strands, and place in the skillet. Season pasta lightly with salt. Add ⅓ cup of the Parmigiano and quickly toss over low heat until the sauce coats the pasta. Add some of the reserved cooking water if pasta seems a bit dry. Taste, adjust the seasoning, and serve with additional Parmigiano.

SERVES 4 TO 6

BUTTER, SAGE, RICOTTA, AND PARMIGIANO

BURRO, SALVIA, RICOTTA E PARMIGIANO

This dish reflects the simplicity of old peasant-style Italian cooking when dishes were prepared with whatever ingredients one had at hand. When I tested this dish, I used a superlative ricotta from San Francisco and a Parmigiano-Reggiano from my home region of Emilia-Romagna. Check your local Italian market for the best cheeses you can get.

1 pound spaghetti

6 tablespoons unsalted butter

6 to 8 fresh sage leaves, shredded

½ pound ricotta cheese or goat cheese

1½ cups whole milk

⅓ to ½ cup freshly grated Parmigiano-Reggiano cheese

Salt and freshly ground pepper, to taste

1 Cook spaghetti in boiling salted water according to package directions. When pasta is almost done, scoop up and reserve ½ cup of the cooking water.

2 Meanwhile, heat the butter in a small skillet, add the sage, and stir for a minute or two. Place butter and sage in a large warm bowl that can later accommodate the pasta.

3 Add the ricotta, milk, and Parmigiano to the bowl and season with salt and pepper. Mix the ingredients thoroughly with a large spoon until you have a soft, loose mixture. If your mixture is too thick, add a bit more milk or pasta cooking water.

4 Drain spaghetti, leaving just a little bit of water attached to its strands, and place in the bowl. Mix well, taste, and adjust the seasoning if needed, and serve at once.

SERVES 4 TO 6

FRESH TOMATO SAUCE WITH RICOTTA CHEESE AND BASIL

SUGO DI POMODORO E RICOTTA

This is one of the simplest and most delicious summer tomato sauces—fragrant ripe tomatoes, a bit of garlic, a handful of green basil, and a small amount of ricotta or goat cheese. The addition of cheese gives the sauce a sweeter taste.

2 pounds juicy ripe tomatoes

⅓ cup extra virgin olive oil, more if needed

2 cloves garlic, peeled and smashed

Salt and freshly ground pepper, to taste

½ cup ricotta cheese or goat cheese

1 cup loosely packed shredded fresh basil

1 pound spaghetti

1 Bring a large pot of water to a boil. Add the tomatoes and simmer until the skin begins to split. Transfer tomatoes to a bowl of cold water and remove the skin. Cut tomatoes in half and remove the seeds and then cut into chunks and purée through a food mill or in a food processor.

2 Heat the oil in a medium-size saucepan on medium heat. Add the garlic and cook until it is golden and soft. Discard the garlic. Add the tomatoes, season with salt and pepper, and cook, uncovered over medium heat, for 10 to 12 minutes or until the sauce begins to thicken. Add the ricotta and stir until it is dissolved. Add the basil, stir once or twice, and turn off the heat.

3 Meanwhile, cook spaghetti in boiling salted water according to package directions.

4 Put half of the tomato sauce in a large warm serving bowl. Drain pasta, add to the bowl, and stir to combine. Serve with a little more sauce, if you wish.

SERVES 4 TO 6

FRESH AND SUN-DRIED TOMATOES WITH PECORINO CHEESE

POMODORI CON AGLIO, PEPERONCINO E PECORINO

This is a delightful and very appetizing sauce that one can find in the trattorie of Southern Italy. The pasta can be spaghetti, large rigatoni, or shells and the cheese is generally Pecorino Romano, a great Roman cheese.

½ cup extra virgin olive oil

2 pounds ripe plum tomatoes, peeled, seeded, and diced

2 tablespoons oil-packed sun-dried tomatoes, minced

2 cloves garlic, chopped

Salt, to taste

Chopped fresh red chili pepper or hot red pepper flakes, to taste

2 tablespoons minced parsley

1 pound spaghetti

1 cup grated Pecorino Romano cheese or Parmigiano-Reggiano cheese

1 Heat the oil in a large skillet over medium heat. Add the plum tomatoes and cook, stirring, for 3 to 4 minutes. Add the sun-dried tomatoes, garlic, salt, and chili pepper and stir for a minute or two.

2 Reduce the heat to medium low and simmer 3 to 4 minutes, stirring the sauce a few times. Stir in the parsley during the last two minutes of cooking and turn off the heat.

3 Meanwhile, cook spaghetti in boiling salted water according to package directions. Drain spaghetti and add to the skillet and mix until pasta and sauce are well combined. Place the pasta into individual bowls, sprinkle generously with cheese, and serve.

SERVES 4 TO 6

MOZZARELLA, CHERRY TOMATOES, AND BASIL CAPRI STYLE

SPAGHETTI CON BUFALO MOZZARELLA, POMODORINI E BASILICO

Ripe tomatoes, mozzarella, olive oil, fresh herbs, and spaghetti are synonymous with the food of Naples and the Campania region. On cool days, this delicious sauce is generally briefly cooked and served while hot. On warmer days, the same ingredients are mixed together into a large serving bowl and served at room temperature. The pasta is cooked and added to the hot or cool ingredients.

½ cup extra virgin olive oil

2 pounds cherry tomatoes washed, dried, and cut in half

Salt and freshly ground pepper, to taste

2 cloves garlic, minced

10 to 12 basil leaves, shredded

1 pound spaghetti

½ pound mozzarella di Bufala or whole cow's milk mozzarella, diced

1 Heat the oil in a large skillet over medium heat. Add the tomatoes, season with salt and pepper, and stir until tomatoes begin to soften, 3 to 4 minutes. Add the garlic and basil and stir for 1 to 2 minutes.

2 Meanwhile, cook spaghetti in boiling salted water according to package directions.

3 Drain spaghetti and add to the skillet and add the mozzarella. Briefly mix until mozzarella begins to soften, 1 to 2 minutes. Taste, adjust the seasoning, and serve.

SERVES 4 TO 6

PANCETTA, EGGS, PARMIGIANO, AND MASCARPONE CHEESE

PANCETTA, UOVA, PARMIGIANO E MASCARPONE

One of my very favorite pasta dishes is spaghetti alla Carbonara, made with raw eggs, bacon, and Parmigiano. One night when my grandchildren came over for dinner I stirred a few ounces of mascarpone that I happened to have in my refrigerator into the eggs and Parmigiano. The sweetness of the mascarpone cheese paired with the more assertive ingredients made this dish so appetizing that no one at the table talked until the pasta on their plate was gone.

1 pound spaghetti

2 whole eggs

2 egg yolks

1 cup mascarpone cheese (about 5 ounces)

¾ cup freshly grated Parmigiano-Reggiano cheese, divided

Salt and freshly ground pepper, to taste

2 tablespoons extra virgin olive oil

¼ pound thickly sliced pancetta, cut into 1-inch dice

1 Cook spaghetti in boiling salted water according to package directions.

2 Meanwhile, in a large warm bowl that can later accommodate the pasta, add the eggs, mascarpone, and half of the Parmigiano. Season with salt and a generous amount of pepper and mix well to combine.

3 Heat the oil in a large skillet. Add the pancetta and stir over medium heat until just barely golden, about 1 minute.

4 Drain spaghetti, leaving just a little bit of water attached to its strands, and add to the skillet. Stir until pasta is well coated with the oil and pancetta. Add the contents of the skillet into the bowl and mix well to combine. Taste, adjust the seasonings, and serve with a sprinkle of Parmigiano.

NOTE: When raw eggs are stirred in a warm bowl with a hot pasta, they are semicooked by the heat. Make sure to buy the freshest eggs possible.

SERVES 4 TO 6

PANCETTA, HOT PEPPER, OLIVE OIL, AND PECORINO

PANCETTA, PEPERONCINO, OLIO DI OLIVA E PECORINO

This is a typical dish of Rome; a dish that peasants, laborers, and well-to-do people all seem to totally love. This is also one of the first dishes I order when I arrive in Rome. Because the sauce can be made in the time the pasta cooks, prepare the ingredients ahead of time, and then dazzle your family or friends with this quintessential Roman dish.

1 pound spaghetti

⅓ cup extra virgin olive oil

4 tablespoons unsalted butter

1 cup minced yellow onion

6 ounces thickly sliced pancetta, diced

2 cloves garlic, minced

A generous pinch of hot red pepper flakes

2 tablespoons chopped fresh parsley

1 cup grated Pecorino Romano cheese, divided

Salt, to taste

1 Cook spaghetti in boiling salted water according to package directions. When pasta is almost done, scoop up and reserve ½ cup of the cooking water.

2 Meanwhile, heat the oil and butter in a large skillet over medium heat. Add the onion and stir until it is pale yellow and soft then add the pancetta. Stir gently until pancetta is lightly golden. Add the garlic and red pepper flakes and stir for about 1 minute. Turn off the heat.

3 Drain spaghetti, leaving just a little water attached to its strands, and place in the skillet. Toss spaghetti with the sauce, parsley, ⅓ cup of the Pecorino Romano cheese, and season lightly with salt. Mix over low heat until pasta is well coated. Add some of the reserved pasta water if needed. Taste and adjust the seasoning. Serve piping hot with a bit more cheese, if desired.

SERVES 4 TO 6

PANCETTA, EGGS, PEAS, AND PARMIGIANO

PANCETTA, UOVA, PISELLI E PARMIGIANO

Spaghetti with pancetta, eggs, and cheese is a traditional Roman dish—one that is quite famous in many parts of the world today. Here, the golden pancetta, eggs, and Parmigiano cheese have the addition of fresh peas which bestow additional flavor on an already great dish.

3 whole eggs

2 egg yolks

1 cup freshly grated Parmigiano-Reggiano cheese, divided

Salt and freshly ground pepper, to taste

1 pound spaghetti

1/3 cup extra virgin olive oil

1/4 pound thickly sliced pancetta, cut into 1/2-inch dice

1 cup fresh shelled peas, parboiled, or thawed frozen peas

1 In a large warm bowl that can later accommodate the pasta, beat the eggs with the yolks and 1/2 cup of the Parmigiano cheese. Season with salt and a generous amount of pepper and set aside.

2 Meanwhile, cook spaghetti in boiling salted water according to package directions.

3 While the pasta is cooking, warm the oil in a small skillet over medium heat. Add the pancetta and stir until lightly golden. Add the peas and stir for 1 or 2 minutes or until they are heated through. Turn off the heat under the skillet.

4 Drain pasta and place in the bowl with the eggs. Add the pancetta-pea sauce and a little more Parmigiano. Quickly mix until pasta is thickly coated with the sauce. Taste, adjust the seasoning, and serve with additional cheese, if desired.

SERVES 4 TO 6

PROSCIUTTO, CREAM, AND SWISS CHEESE

PROSCIUTTO DI PARMA, PANNA E FORMAGGIO SVIZZERO

This is another rich dish that most of us crave every once in a while. However, if your portions are very small, there's no reason why you can't enjoy it. Make sure to add the swiss cheese after removing the pasta from the heat so it will become softer, but not lumpy.

1 pound spaghetti

5 tablespoons unsalted butter

5 ounces thickly sliced prosciutto, cut into small dice

1 cup heavy cream

Grated rind of 1 lemon

1 to 2 tablespoons of freshly chopped parsley

Salt and freshly grated pepper, to taste

1 cup diced Swiss cheese

1 Cook spaghetti in boiling salted water according to package directions. When pasta is almost done, scoop up and reserve ½ cup of the cooking water.

2 Meanwhile, heat the butter in a large skillet over medium heat. As soon as the butter begins to foam, add the prosciutto and stir until it is lightly golden, about 1 minute. Add the cream, lemon rind, parsley, and the reserved cooking water. Stir over medium-low heat until the sauce has a medium-thick consistency, 1 to 2 minutes. Lightly season with salt and several twists of black pepper. Turn off the heat.

3 Drain pasta, leaving just a little water attached to its strands, and place in the skillet. Add the Swiss cheese and mix well to combine. Taste, adjust the seasoning, and serve.

SERVES 4 TO 6

PECORINO ROMANO CHEESE, PEPPER, AND CRISP GARLIC

CACIO, PEPE E AGLIO CROOCCANTE

This is the simplest, tastiest pasta dish of Rome and is a staple of the many Roman trattorie. It is a dish that uses great Pecorino Romano cheese with abandon and lots of pepper. Today, this dish has several variations as in this recipe which uses fresh garlic.

½ cup extra virgin olive oil

4 large cloves garlic, peeled and thinly sliced

Salt and freshly ground pepper, to taste

1 pound spaghetti

1 cup grated Pecorino Romano cheese, divided

1 Heat the oil in a small saucepan, add the garlic, and stir over low heat until golden taking care not to burn the garlic. Season the oil with salt and several twists of pepper. Turn off the heat under the saucepan.

2 Meanwhile, cook spaghetti in boiling salted water according to the package directions. Scoop up and reserve ½ cup of the cooking water.

3 Drain spaghetti and discard the water. Place spaghetti back into the hot pot; add the contents of the saucepan and ½ cup of the cheese. Stir in the reserved pasta water and quickly toss. Taste and adjust the seasoning. Serve with a little more Pecorino Romano cheese.

SERVES 4 TO 6

PROSCIUTTO, BUTTER, SAGE, AND PARMIGIANO

PROSCIUTTO, BURRO, SALVIA E PARMIGIANO

This sauce is typically served over homemade tagliatelle, but because my grandchildren simply love spaghetti, I decided to use this very good, very fast sauce during one of our Sunday dinners. It was a hit!

1 pound spaghetti

7 tablespoons unsalted butter

5 ounces thickly sliced prosciutto, diced

10 to 12 fresh sage leaves, shredded

Salt, to taste

1 cup freshly grated Parmigiano-Reggiano cheese, divided

1 Cook spaghetti in boiling salted water according to package directions. When pasta is almost done, scoop up and reserve ½ cup of the cooking water.

2 Meanwhile, heat the butter in a small saucepan over medium heat. Add prosciutto and sage and stir until prosciutto has a light golden color, 1 to 2 minutes. Add the reserved cooking water, season with salt, and stir until sauce has a thicker consistency.

3 Drain pasta and place in a large warm serving bowl. Add the prosciutto-butter sauce, half of the Parmigiano, and mix well to combine. Taste, adjust the seasoning, and serve with a little more Parmigiano, if desired.

SERVE 4 TO 6

SMOKED MOZZARELLA, SUN-DRIED TOMATOES, CAPERS, AND HERBS

MOZZARELLA AFFUMICATA, POMODORINI, CAPPERI E ERBETTE

Smoked mozzarella should be only briefly tossed with the pasta and its sauce. If allowed to cook too long, the mozzarella will clump.

1 pound spaghetti

½ cup extra virgin olive oil

3 cloves garlic, minced

½ cup minced green olives

½ cup capers, rinsed and patted dry

⅓ cup minced oil-packed sun-dried tomatoes

Salt and freshly ground pepper, to taste

½ cup loosely packed minced fresh herbs (basil, oregano, thyme, parsley, sage)

4 ounces grated smoked mozzarella

1 Cook spaghetti in boiling salted water according to package directions. When pasta is almost done, scoop up and reserve ½ cup of the cooking water.

2 Meanwhile, heat the oil in a large skillet over medium heat. Add the garlic, olives, capers, and tomatoes and stir for 1 to 2 minutes. Lightly season with salt and a generous amount of pepper.

3 Drain the pasta and place in the skillet. Add the reserved cooking water, fresh herbs, and mozzarella. Stir quickly until the cheese just begins to soften, 1 to 2 minutes. Turn off the heat, taste and adjust the seasoning, and serve.

SERVES 4 TO 6

SMOKED PANCETTA, HOT PEPPER, SAFFRON, AND PECORINO CHEESE

PANCETTA AFFUMICATA, PEPERONCINO, ZAFFERANO E PECORINO

When a sauce is made with only a handful of ingredients, Italian cooks add a bit of starchy pasta water to the skillet, which in cooking down, ties the ingredients together and moistens the pasta.

⅓ cup extra virgin olive oil

3 tablespoons unsalted butter

5 ounces thickly sliced smoked pancetta, cut into small dice

Hot red pepper flakes, to taste

1 pound spaghetti

¼ teaspoon powdered saffron

1 to 2 tablespoons chopped fresh parsley

½ cup of freshly grated Pecorino Romano cheese, divided

1 Heat the oil and butter in a large skillet over medium heat. When the skillet is hot, add the pancetta and red pepper flakes and cook, stirring until pancetta is lightly golden, about 2 minutes.

2 Meanwhile, cook spaghetti in boiling salted water according to package directions. When pasta is almost done, scoop up ½ cup of the cooking water and whisk with the saffron in a small bowl; stir into the skillet.

3 Drain pasta and add to the skillet. Stir in the parsley and about half of the cheese. Mix over low heat until pasta is well coated with the sauce. Taste and adjust the seasoning and serve with remaining Pecorino cheese.

SERVES 4 TO 6

TALEGGIO, CREAM, AND PARMIGIANO
TALEGGIO CREMA E PARMIGIANO

Taleggio, a whole cow's milk cheese typical of the region of Lombardy, has a mild, sweet, and creamy taste. This sinfully rich dish is not the lightest pasta in the world. For this reason, I suggest that you use it in moderation, serving it in small amounts—unless you have a husband like mine who cleaned his plate and said, "Great, can I have a little more?"

1 pound spaghetti

4 tablespoons unsalted butter

1½ cups heavy cream

6 ounces Taleggio cheese, cut into medium-size pieces

Salt, to taste

Paprika, to taste

½ cup freshly grated Parmigiano-Reggiano cheese

1 Cook spaghetti in boiling salted water according to package directions.

2 While the pasta is cooking, heat the butter in a large skillet over medium heat. Add the cream and the Taleggio cheese, lightly season with salt, and stir until the cheese has melted and the sauce begins to thicken, 2 to 3 minutes. Stir in a little paprika and turn off the heat.

3 When pasta is almost done, scoop up and reserve ½ cup of the cooking water.

4 Drain pasta and place in the skillet. Quickly stir over medium-low heat until pasta and sauce are well combined. Add a little of the reserved cooking water if sauce is too thick. Serve at once with a sprinkle of Parmigiano.

SERVES 4 TO 6

UNCOOKED TOMATOES, MOZZARELLA, AND BASIL CAPRI STYLE

SPAGHETTI WITH BUFALO MOZZARELLA, POMODORO E BASILICO

This is a classic Southern Italian dish that serves an uncooked summer tomato sauce over spaghetti. Often, there is the addition of mozzarella which is added to the sauce just before serving. The heat of the pasta is just enough to soften the mozzarella.

2 pounds fresh tomatoes

2 cloves garlic, minced

8 to 10 basil leaves, shredded

6 springs fresh oregano

4 to 5 oil-packed anchovy filets, minced

½ cup extra virgin olive oil

Salt and freshly ground pepper, to taste

1 pound spaghetti

½ pound fresh whole milk mozzarella, diced

1 Peel the tomatoes by making a cross at the bottom end of the tomatoes and drop them into boiling water. Boil until their skins split, 1 to 2 minutes. Transfer the tomatoes to a bowl of ice water. When cool, pat dry and peel off their skins. Seed and dice the tomatoes and place in a strainer over a bowl to release some of their juice.

2 Put the tomatoes into a large serving bowl, add the garlic, basil, oregano, and anchovies. Add the oil, season with salt and pepper, and stir ingredients well. Taste and adjust the seasoning.

3 Meanwhile, cook spaghetti in boiling salted water according to package directions.

4 Drain pasta, place in the serving bowl, and toss to combine. Add the mozzarella and stir until it just begins to soften. Sprinkle with a little more oil if needed. Taste, adjust the seasoning, and serve.

SERVES 4 TO 6

WALNUT-GORGONZOLA SAUCE

SALSA DI NOCI E GORGONZOLA

This is the type of dish I love to cook because it is very quick and very good. While the spaghetti is cooking, the sauce simmers very gently on low heat. If the sauce thickens too much, scoop up a little pasta water and stir into the sauce, then serve immediately.

½ cup shelled walnuts

Olive oil

1 pound spaghetti

4 tablespoons unsalted butter

1 cup heavy cream

3 ounces mild sweet Gorgonzola cheese, cut into small pieces

Salt, to taste

1 Preheat oven to 350 F. Scatter the walnuts on a lightly oiled baking sheet and place in the oven. Roast until walnuts are lightly golden, about 2 minutes. Remove from oven and place in the bowl of a food processor and pulse the machine on and off until walnuts are finely chopped. Transfer to a small bowl until ready to use.

2 Meanwhile, cook spaghetti in boiling salted water according to package directions.

3 As the spaghetti is cooking, heat the butter in a large skillet over medium heat. When the butter begins to foam, add walnuts and stir once or twice. Add the cream and Gorgonzola and lightly season with salt. Reduce the heat to low and simmer, stirring occasionally, until sauce has a medium-thick consistency, about 2 to 3 minutes. Turn off the heat.

4 When pasta is almost done, scoop up ½ cup of the cooking water and set aside. Drain pasta and place in the skillet with the sauce. Briefly mix over low heat until pasta and sauce are well combined. Add a little of the reserved cooking water if pasta seems a bit dry. Taste, adjust the seasoning, and serve.

SERVES 4 TO 6

PESTO

32 Basil-Pine Nut Pesto Ligurian Style

34 Basil Pesto with Broccoli

36 Basil, Walnut, and Sun-Dried Tomato Pesto

37 Creamy Walnut, Ricotta, Basil, and Arugula Pesto

38 Basil-Olive Pesto and Cherry Tomatoes

40 Mediterranean Pesto with Tomatoes

42 Pesto and Goat Cheese

43 Pesto, Peas, and Asparagus

44 Pesto of Olives, Sun-Dried Tomatoes, Capers, and Arugula

45 Pesto and Potatoes

BASIL-PINE NUT PESTO LIGURIAN STYLE

PESTO ALLA GENOVESE

One of the blessings of spring and summer is the abundance of basil—and with basil, you make pesto. Making pesto is quite easy and you probably will never buy pesto in a jar again.

2 cups tightly packed basil leaves without stems

2 cloves garlic, peeled

4 tablespoons pine nuts

Salt, to taste

½ cup extra virgin olive oil, divided

⅓ cup freshly grated Parmigiano-Reggiano cheese

⅓ cup freshly grated Pecorino Romano cheese

1 pound spaghetti

1 Place the basil, garlic, pine nuts, salt, and about half of the oil in the bowl of a food processor or a blender. Turn the machine on and off several times until the mixture turns into a soft paste. Add the remaining oil, Parmigiano, and Pecorino and process until the mixture is smooth and creamy. Taste and adjust the seasoning. Transfer pesto to a bowl, cover, and set aside.

2 Meanwhile, cook spaghetti in boiling salted water according to package directions.

3 When pasta is almost done, scoop up and reserve ½ cup of the cooking water. Drain the pasta and place in a large warm bowl. Toss with half of the pesto and a few tablespoons of the reserved cooking water or a little olive oil. Taste and adjust the seasoning and serve with a little more Parmigiano or Pecorino if needed.

SERVES 4 TO 6

BASIL PESTO WITH BROCCOLI

PESTO DI BASILICO CON BROCCOLI

If you are a vegetarian, this dish is for you. Occasionally I want to eat only pasta and vegetables and this fits the bill. Of course, it tastes even better if you drink it with a nice glass of white wine.

1 recipe Basil-Pine Nut Pesto Ligurian Style (see page 32)

1 cup broccoli florets

3 tablespoons extra virgin olive oil

Salt, to taste

1 pound spaghetti

½ cup freshly grated Parmigiano-Reggiano cheese, divided

1 Prepare the Basil-Pine Nut Pesto and set aside.

2 Bring a medium pot of salted water to a boil. Add the broccoli florets and cook until tender, 4 to 5 minutes. Drain broccoli, place on a cutting board, and chop into very small pieces.

3 Place the broccoli into a large pasta bowl; add about half of the pesto and the oil. Mix well, taste, and adjust the seasoning.

4 Meanwhile, cook spaghetti in boiling salted water according to package directions.

5 When the pasta is almost done, scoop up and reserve ½ cup of the cooking water. Drain the pasta, place in the bowl, and toss it with the broccoli-pesto mixture and half of the Parmigiano. Stir well to combine. If pasta seems a bit dry, add a little more pesto or a few tablespoons of the reserved cooking water. Serve with additional cheese.

SERVES 4 TO 6

BASIL, WALNUT, AND SUN-DRIED TOMATO PESTO

PESTO DI NOCI E POMODORI SECCHI

I just love spring and summer because of the many varieties of basil pesto. Originally, the classic Ligurian pesto was made simply with fresh basil, pine nuts, garlic, and extra virgin olive oil. Today, however, pesto takes on many faces as you can see in this chapter.

⅓ cup walnuts

⅓ cup sun-dried tomatoes

2 cloves garlic, peeled

3 cups tightly packed basil leaves, without stems

Salt, to taste

½ cup extra virgin olive oil, divided

¾ cup freshly grated Parmigiano-Reggiano cheese, divided

1 pound spaghetti

1 Place walnuts, tomatoes, garlic, basil, salt, and half of the oil in the bowl of a food processor and pulse until mixture is finely minced. Add ½ cup of the cheese and the remaining oil and process until pesto has a smooth, creamy consistency. Taste and adjust the seasoning. Transfer pesto to a bowl. It can be used immediately or covered and refrigerated.

2 Meanwhile, cook spaghetti in boiling salted water according to package directions.

3 When pasta is almost done, scoop up and reserve ½ cup of the cooking water. Drain the pasta, place in a large warm bowl, and toss with half the pesto. If pasta seems a bit dry, add a little more pesto and a few tablespoons of the reserved cooking water. Taste and adjust the seasoning and serve with a sprinkle of Parmigiano cheese.

SERVES 4 TO 6

CREAMY WALNUT, RICOTTA, BASIL, AND ARUGULA PESTO

PESTO DI NOCI, RICOTTA, BASILICO E RUCOLA

This simple pesto uses walnuts instead of pine nuts, mixes arugula with basil, and stirs together the milk and ricotta cheese. The result is a light creamy pesto that coats the spaghetti quite well.

⅓ cup walnuts, roughly chopped

1 cup basil leaves without stems

1 cup arugula

2 cloves garlic

½ cup extra virgin olive oil, divided

Salt, to taste

⅓ cup heavy cream

⅓ cup ricotta cheese

½ cup grated Parmigiano-Reggiano cheese, divided

1 pound spaghetti

1 Place the walnuts, basil, arugula, garlic, half of the oil, and salt in the bowl of a food processor and process until the mixture is smooth. Add the cream, ricotta, and ⅓ cup of Parmigiano and process on and off until mixture is smooth and creamy. Transfer pesto to a bowl, taste, and adjust the seasoning.

2 Meanwhile, cook spaghetti in boiling salted water according to package directions.

3 When pasta is almost done, scoop up and reserve ½ cup of the cooking water. Drain the pasta, place in a large bowl, and toss with about half of the pesto and the remaining Parmigiano. Taste and adjust the seasoning. If pasta seems too dry, add a little more pesto, a few tablespoons of the reserved cooking water, or the remaining oil. Serve at once.

SERVES 4 TO 6

BASIL-OLIVE PESTO AND CHERRY TOMATOES

PESTO DI OLIVE E POMODORINI

Several years ago on the Adriatic coast of Emilia-Romagna, I was served a basil-olive pesto topped by bright diced tomatoes. When I asked the server why they put the tomatoes over this classic sauce, he simply said, "Because we tried it and we liked it."

BASIL-OLIVE PESTO

½ cup black olives, pitted and halved

2 cups tightly packed basil leaves

2 cloves garlic, peeled

4 tablespoons pine nuts

½ cup extra virgin olive oil, divided

½ cup freshly grated Parmigiano-Reggiano cheese, divided

Salt, to taste

TOMATOES

⅓ cup extra virgin olive oil

½ pound ripe cherry tomatoes, halved

Salt, to taste

1 pound spaghetti

1 To make the pesto; place the olives, basil, garlic, pine nuts, and half of the oil in the bowl of a food processor. Turn the machine on and off several times until mixture turns into a paste. Add the remaining oil, half of the Parmigiano, lightly season with salt, and process until the mixture is smooth and creamy. Transfer pesto to a bowl, cover, and set aside until ready to use. If you don't plan to use pesto within a few hours, drizzle 1 tablespoon of olive oil over the top to prevent discoloration. Cover the bowl and refrigerate until ready to use.

2 To prepare the tomatoes; heat the oil in a large skillet over medium-high heat. Add the tomatoes, season with salt, and cook, stirring until tomatoes begin to soften, 3 to 4 minutes. Put tomatoes in a large warm serving bowl, add about ½ cup of pesto, and mix well.

3 Meanwhile, cook spaghetti in boiling salted water according to package directions.

4 When pasta is almost done, scoop up and reserve ½ a cup of the cooking water. Drain spaghetti, place in the bowl with the pesto and tomatoes, and toss to combine. Add a few tablespoons of the reserved cooking water, if needed. Serve at once with the remaining Parmigiano.

SERVES 4 TO 6

MEDITERRANEAN PESTO WITH TOMATOES

PESTO ALLA MEDITERRANEA

This is a classic basil pesto that has the reinforcement of ripe summer tomatoes. The green of the pesto and the red of the tomatoes make this pasta sauce fragrant and visually appealing.

1 recipe Basil-Pine Nut Pesto Ligurian style, (see page 32)

½ pound ripe tomatoes

Salt, to taste

¼ cup extra virgin olive oil

1 pound spaghetti

⅓ cup freshly grated Parmigiano-Reggiano cheese, divided

⅓ cup grated Pecorino Romano cheese, divided

1 Prepare the Basil-Pine Nut Pesto and set aside.

2 Bring a large pot of salted water to a boil. Cut a cross at the bottom end of each tomato and drop them into boiling water. Boil tomatoes until their skin begins to split, 1 to 2 minutes. Drain and chill tomatoes in cold water. Peel tomatoes and remove the seeds. Mince and place them in a colander for about 1 hour to drain the watery juices.

3 Place tomatoes in a medium bowl, lightly season with salt, and sprinkle with oil. Add 1 cup of pesto, about half of the Parmigiano, and half of Pecorino and stir well to combine. Taste, adjust the seasoning, and set aside.

4 Meanwhile, cook spaghetti in boiling salted water according to package directions. Drain the pasta and place in a large warm bowl. Add about half of the pesto-tomato sauce, stir well, taste and adjust the seasoning. Add a little more sauce if needed. Serve with just a sprinkle of cheese.

SERVES 4 TO 6

PESTO AND GOAT CHEESE

PESTO CON RICOTTA DI CAPRA

The addition of creamy goat cheese to classic pesto gives it a smooth delicate texture and a very appetizing look.

2 cups tightly packed basil leaves

4 tablespoons pine nuts

2 cloves garlic, peeled

½ cup extra virgin olive oil

Salt, to taste

5 ounces goat cheese

1 pound spaghetti

½ cup freshly grated Parmigiano-Reggiano cheese

1 Place the basil, pine nuts, garlic, oil, and salt in the bowl of a food processor and process until smooth. Add the goat cheese and turn the processor on and off until the mixture has a smooth creamy consistency. Taste and adjust the seasoning. Transfer pesto to a bowl, cover, and refrigerate until ready to use.

2 Meanwhile, cook spaghetti in boiling salted water according to package directions.

3 When pasta is almost done, scoop up and reserve ½ cup of the cooking water. Drain the pasta and place in a large warm bowl. Toss it with half the pesto and a few tablespoons of the reserved cooking water or a little olive oil if needed. Taste and adjust the seasoning and serve with a sprinkle of Parmigiano.

SERVES 4 TO 6

PESTO, PEAS, AND ASPARAGUS

PESTO CON PISELLI E ASPARAGI

This is one of those springtime pasta dishes that is not only beautiful to look at, but is also light and delicious. Try not to over use the pesto because a little of this assertive sauce goes a long way.

1 recipe Basil-Pine Nut
Pesto (see page 32)

1 pound spaghetti

1 cup fresh peas or thawed frozen peas

1 cup fresh asparagus tips
or frozen asparagus tips

½ cup freshly grated Parmigiano-
Reggiano cheese

1 Prepare the Basil-Pine Nut Pesto and set aside.

2 Meanwhile, cook spaghetti in boiling salted water until it is cooked half way through. Add the fresh peas and the asparagus tips and stir until the vegetables and the spaghetti are cooked but still a bit firm to the bite. (If you are using frozen vegetables, add them to the pot 1 or 2 minutes before draining the pasta.)

3 When pasta is almost done, scoop up and reserve about ½ cup of the cooking water. Drain the pasta and vegetables and place them in a large warm bowl. Add enough pesto to coat the pasta and a nice sprinkling of Parmigiano. Add a few tablespoons of the reserved cooking water or a little olive oil if sauce looks too dry. Toss everything, taste and adjust the seasoning, and serve at once.

SERVES 4 TO 6

PESTO OF OLIVES, SUN-DRIED TOMATOES, CAPERS, AND ARUGULA

PESTO DI OLIVE, POMODORINI SECCHI, CAPPERI E RUGOLA

Pesto is extremely easy to make. The only things you need are a food processor, fresh seasonal ingredients, great olive oil, and superlative cheese—and in no time at all you will have a great pasta dish on the table.

2 tablespoons black olive paste or 10 pitted black olives, diced

⅓ cup sun-dried tomatoes

2 tablespoons capers, rinsed

2 anchovy filets

2 cloves garlic

2 cups arugula

½ cup extra virgin olive oil

½ cup freshly grated Parmigiano-Reggiano cheese, divided

Hot red pepper flakes, to taste

Salt, to taste

1 pound spaghetti

1 Combine the olive paste or olives, tomatoes, capers, anchovies, garlic, and arugula in the bowl of a food processor. Add the oil and turn the machine on and off several times until the mixture turns into a soft paste. Add ⅓ cup of the Parmigiano and process until mixture is smooth and creamy. Place the mixture in a bowl and sprinkle with some red pepper flakes and salt. If pesto is too thick, add a little bit of olive oil. If pesto is too thin, stir in the remaining Parmigiano.

2 Meanwhile, cook spaghetti in boiling salted water according to package directions.

3 When pasta is almost done, scoop up and reserve ½ cup of the cooking water. Drain the pasta, place in a large bowl, and toss with half the pesto. If pasta seems a bit dry, add a little more pesto and a few tablespoons of the reserved cooking water. Taste and adjust the seasoning and serve with a sprinkle of Parmigiano.

SERVES 4 TO 6

PESTO AND POTATOES

PESTO CON PATATE

When the basil is seasonally fresh, buy it and make a large batch of pesto. You can freeze what you don't use. Make sure to coat the top of the pesto with a little olive oil before you freeze it. The oil will prevent the top of the pesto from becoming dark.

1 recipe Basil-Pine Nut
Pesto (see page 32)

6 ounces Yukon gold potatoes, peeled,
and cut into ½-inch dice (about 1 cup)

1 pound spaghetti

¾ cup freshly grated Parmigiano-
Reggiano cheese, divided

1 Prepare the Basil-Pine Nut Pesto and set aside.

2 Bring a medium pot of salted water to a boil. Add the potatoes and cook until tender, 5 to 6 minutes. Drain and set aside.

3 Meanwhile, cook spaghetti in boiling salted water according to package directions.

4 When pasta is almost done, scoop up and reserve ½ cup of the cooking water. Drain the pasta, place in a large warm bowl, and toss it with half the pesto, the potatoes, half of the Parmigiano, and a few tablespoons of the reserved cooking water. Add a little more pesto if needed. Taste and adjust the seasoning and serve at once with a sprinkle of cheese.

SERVES 4 TO 6

QUICK TOMATO

48 Arugula, Tomatoes, and Peppery Sauce

49 Basic Tomato-Basil Sauce

50 Cherry Tomatoes, Mozzarella, and Herb Salad

51 Tomatoes, Sun-Dried Tomatoes, and Prosciutto

52 Neapolitan Tomato Sauce

53 Tomato Sauce with Goat Cheese and Basil

54 Marinara Sauce

56 Oven-Roasted Tomato Sauce

58 Tomato, Cream, and Hot Pepper

59 Tomato, Cream, and Vodka Sauce

60 Tomatoes, Pancetta, and Hot Pepper Sauce Roman Style

61 Tomatoes, Butter, and Parmigiano

62 Tomatoes, Capers, and Olives

64 Uncooked Summer Tomatoes and Herbs

ARUGULA, TOMATOES, AND PEPPERY SAUCE

RUGOLA, POMODORO E PEPERONCINO

This is comfort food, southern Italian style. Great olive oil, perfect tomatoes, bitter tasting arugula, and a superb Pecorino Romano cheese are transformed into a most delicious sauce in no time at all.

4 cups arugula, washed, dried, and stems removed

½ cup extra virgin olive oil, divided

2 cloves garlic, minced

1 (28-ounce) can whole Italian plum tomatoes, put through a food mill to remove seeds

Salt and hot red pepper flakes, to taste

1 pound spaghetti

½ cup freshly grated Pecorino Romano cheese, divided

1 Place arugula in the bowl of a food processor, add 2 tablespoons of oil, and process until smooth. Set aside.

2 Heat the remaining oil in a medium saucepan over medium heat. Add garlic and stir until it just begins to turn golden. Add the tomatoes, season with salt and red pepper flakes, and simmer over low heat, stirring from time to time, until sauce has a medium-thick consistency, 10 to 12 minutes.

3 Meanwhile, cook spaghetti in boiling salted water according to package directions.

4 While the pasta is cooking, stir the puréed arugula into the sauce. Taste and adjust the seasoning and turn off the heat.

5 Drain pasta and place in a large warm serving bowl. Add half of the sauce and half of the cheese and mix until pasta and sauce are well combined. Add more sauce if needed. Taste, adjust the seasoning, and serve with a sprinkle of additional cheese.

SERVES 4 TO 6

BASIC TOMATO-BASIL SAUCE
SUGO DI POMODORO

This is a basic and delicious tomato sauce that can be used to top not only spaghetti, but also other shapes of pasta such as penne, rigatoni, or fettuccine. I love to make it in large batches, use what I need, and refrigerate or freeze the leftovers.

3 pounds ripe summer tomatoes
½ cup extra virgin olive oil, divided
1 medium onion, diced
1 carrot, peeled and diced
1 celery stick, diced
6 to 8 fresh basil leaves, shredded
Salt, to taste

1 Bring a large pot of water to a boil. Add the tomatoes and simmer until the skin begins to split, about 1 minute. Transfer tomatoes to a bowl of cold water and then remove skins and cut into large pieces. Place in a large bowl and set aside.

2 Heat half of the oil in a large saucepan. Add the tomatoes and their juices, onion, carrot, and celery into the saucepan and bring to a boil. Reduce the heat to low and simmer 25 to 30 minutes, stirring occasionally, until sauce has a nice thick consistency and vegetables are cooked all the way through. Add the basil during the last few minutes of cooking.

3 Put the contents of the saucepan through a food mill and then place back into the saucepan. Season with salt and stir the remaining oil into the sauce. Taste and adjust the seasoning. The sauce can be used immediately or chilled and frozen.

MAKES APPROXIMATELY 4 TO 5 CUPS SAUCE

CHERRY TOMATOES, MOZZARELLA, AND HERB SALAD

POMODORINI CRUDI, MOZZARELLA E ERBETTE

Italians love tomatoes, especially in the summer, when they are fresh, plump, and irresistible. This tomato and pasta salad is a great dish that combines the bounty of summer and takes away the stress of cooking in a hot kitchen.

2 pounds ripe cherry tomatoes

½ cup loosely packed, lightly minced fresh herbs (basil, oregano, parsley, and mint)

2 to 3 tablespoons capers, rinsed and minced

½ pound fresh mozzarella, cut into small dice

Salt and freshly ground pepper, to taste

½ cup extra virgin olive oil

1 to 2 tablespoons aged Balsamic vinegar

1 pound spaghetti

1 Wash the cherry tomatoes, pat them dry, and cut in half. Place tomatoes in a large salad bowl; add the herbs, capers, and mozzarella. Season with salt and a generous amount of pepper then add the oil and vinegar. Stir well to combine.

2 Meanwhile, cook spaghetti in boiling salted water according to package directions.

3 Drain the pasta and place in the bowl with the tomatoes and mozzarella. Stir quickly until pasta and sauce are well combined. Before serving, taste and adjust the seasoning.

SERVES 4 TO 6

TOMATOES, SUN-DRIED TOMATOES, AND PROSCIUTTO

SALSA DI POMODORI FRESCHI E SECCHI

When ripe sweet tomatoes are not available, we have to improvise. So I look for the best tomatoes I can get. Then I combine them with a few tablespoons of minced sun-dried tomatoes imported from Italy, good quality prosciutto, and the best extra virgin olive oil I can find.

⅓ cup extra virgin olive oil

4 ounces thickly sliced prosciutto, diced

⅓ cup oil-packed sun-dried tomatoes, drained and finely minced

3 pounds ripe plum tomatoes, washed, seeded, and diced

Salt and freshly ground pepper, to taste

1 pound spaghetti

2 tablespoons chopped fresh parsley

½ cup freshly grated Parmigiano-Reggiano cheese

1 Heat the oil in a large skillet over medium heat. Add the prosciutto and stir for 1 to 2 minutes. Add the sun-dried tomatoes and fresh tomatoes, season with salt and pepper, and cook, stirring until the juices of the tomatoes begin to thicken, 4 to 6 minutes.

2 Meanwhile, cook spaghetti in boiling salted water according to package directions.

3 Drain pasta and add to the skillet. Quickly toss over low heat until pasta and sauce are well combined. Taste, adjust the seasoning, and serve with a sprinkle of Parmigiano.

SERVE 4 TO 6

NEAPOLITAN TOMATO SAUCE

SALSA DI POMODORO ALLA NAPOLETANA

The choice of ripe summer tomatoes is essential to a great sauce.

3 pounds fresh tomatoes

1 small yellow onion, peeled and minced

1 celery stalk, minced

2 cloves garlic, minced

½ cup extra virgin olive oil, divided

Salt and freshly ground pepper, to taste

6 to 8 basil leaves

1 pound spaghetti

1 Wash, dry, and seed the tomatoes, cut them into large chunks, and put them in a large saucepan. Add the onion, celery, and garlic and about half of the oil. Season with salt and pepper and cook, uncovered, over low heat until tomatoes begin to fall apart and vegetables are soft, about 25 minutes.

2 Purée tomatoes and vegetables through a food mill into a large bowl. Clean the saucepan, add the remaining oil, and return the tomato-vegetable purée to the pan. Over medium heat, simmer gently until sauce has a medium-thick consistency, 4 to 5 minutes. Tear the basil into pieces and add to the pan. Taste, adjust the seasoning, and turn off the heat.

3 Meanwhile, cook spaghetti in boiling salted water according to package directions.

4 Drain pasta and place in a warm serving bowl. Add about half of the sauce. Quickly toss until pasta and sauce are well combined. Taste, adjust the seasoning, and serve with a little more sauce and a drizzle of olive oil, if needed.

SERVES 4 TO 6

TOMATO SAUCE WITH GOAT CHEESE AND BASIL

SUGO DI POMODORO E CAPRINO

This is one of the simplest and most delicious summer tomato sauces—fragrant ripe tomatoes, a bit of garlic, a handful of green basil, and a small amount of ricotta or goat cheese. The addition of cheese gives the sauce a sweeter taste.

3 pounds fresh tomatoes

½ cup extra virgin olive oil

2 cloves garlic, peeled and smashed

Salt and freshly ground pepper, to taste

½ cup ricotta cheese or goat cheese

1 cup loosely packed shredded fresh basil

1 pound spaghetti

1 Bring a large pot of water to a boil. Add the tomatoes and simmer until skin begins to split. Transfer tomatoes to a bowl of cold water and remove the skin. Cut tomatoes in half, remove the seeds, and cut into chunks. Purée through a food mill or in a food processor.

2 Heat the oil in a medium-size saucepan on medium heat. Add the garlic and cook until it is golden and soft. Discard the garlic. Add the tomatoes, season with salt and pepper, and cook, uncovered, over medium heat, for 10 to 12 minutes or until the sauce begins to thicken. Add the cheese and stir quickly to incorporate. Add the basil, stir once or twice, and turn off the heat.

3 Meanwhile, cook spaghetti in boiling salted water according to package directions.

4 Put half of the tomato sauce in a large warm serving bowl. Drain pasta, add to the bowl, and stir to combine. Serve with a little more sauce.

SERVES 4 TO 6

MARINARA SAUCE

SUGO DI POMODORO ALLA MARINARA

This sauce takes its flavor from two powerful ingredients—garlic and anchovies. If you brown the garlic and discard it, only a faint garlic flavor will be left behind. And if you use anchovies in moderation and stir them into the olive oil with a wooden spoon, your sauce will have only a faint flavor of these two ingredients.

⅓ cup extra virgin olive oil

2 cloves garlic, lightly smashed

1 to 2 anchovy filets, finely chopped

1 (28-ounce) can whole Italian plum tomatoes, with juice and put through a food mill to remove seeds

Salt and freshly ground pepper, to taste

⅓ cup loosely packed fresh oregano leaves

A handful of fresh basil leaves, shredded

1 pound spaghetti

Grated Pecorino Romano cheese, to taste

1 Heat the oil in a medium saucepan over medium heat. Add the garlic and brown on all sides. Discard the garlic. Add the anchovies and stir with a wooden spoon, mashing them into the oil. Add the tomatoes, season with salt and a generous amount of pepper, and bring to a gentle simmer. Cook, stirring occasionally, until sauce has a medium-thick consistency, 8 to 10 minutes. Add the oregano and the basil and stir once or twice. Taste, adjust the seasoning, and turn off the heat.

2 Meanwhile, cook spaghetti in boiling salted water according to package directions.

3 Drain pasta and place in a warm serving bowl. Add about half of the sauce. Quickly toss until pasta and sauce are well combined. Add a little more sauce if needed. Serve at once with a sprinkle of cheese.

SERVES 4 TO 6

OVEN-ROASTED TOMATO SAUCE

SUGO DI POMODORI AL FORNO

This is a perfect summer dish that takes no time at all to put together. Basil can be used instead of oregano.

3½ to 4 pounds fresh tomatoes

½ cup extra virgin olive oil

Salt and freshly ground pepper, to taste

2 cloves garlic, minced

⅓ cup fresh oregano leaves or ¼ teaspoon dried oregano

1 pound spaghetti

½ cup freshly grated Pecorino Romano cheese or Parmigiano-Reggiano cheese

1 Preheat oven to 300 F.

2 Wash and cut tomatoes into large chunks and place them in a large bowl. Toss with oil and season with salt and pepper. Stir in garlic and oregano, toss well, taste, and adjust the seasoning. Spread the mixture on a lightly oiled baking sheet and bake for 15 to 20 minutes until tomatoes have softened and have a somewhat shriveled texture.

3 Remove from oven.

4 Meanwhile, cook spaghetti in boiling salted water according to package directions.

5 Drain pasta and place in a warm serving bowl. Add the tomatoes and toss to combine. Add a little more olive oil, if needed, and serve with a generous sprinkle of cheese.

SERVES 4 TO 6

TOMATO, CREAM, AND HOT PEPPER

POMODORO, PANNA E PEPERONCINO

Tomatoes, butter, and cream cooked for a short time produce a sauce that is savory, sweet, and satisfying. While this sauce marries well with homemade pasta, it is equally delicious on spaghetti and other factory made pasta.

2 tablespoons unsalted butter

2 tablespoons extra virgin olive oil

2 cloves garlic, crushed

1 (28-ounce) can whole Italian plum tomatoes, with juice and put through a food mill to remove seeds

Salt and hot red pepper flakes, to taste

⅓ cup heavy cream

2 to 3 tablespoons chopped fresh parsley

1 pound spaghetti

½ cup freshly grated Parmigiano-Reggiano cheese

1 Heat the butter and the oil in large skillet over medium heat. Add the garlic and stir with a wooden spoon until garlic is golden brown. Discard the garlic. Add the tomatoes, season with salt and red pepper flakes, and cook over medium-low heat, stirring for 6 to 8 minutes. Add the cream and parsley, reduce the heat to medium low, and simmer until the sauce begins to thicken, 2 to 3 minutes. Taste, adjust the seasoning, and turn off the heat.

2 Meanwhile, cook spaghetti in boiling salted water according to package directions.

3 Drain pasta and add to the skillet. Quickly toss over low heat until pasta and sauce are well combined. Taste, adjust the seasoning, and serve with a sprinkle of cheese.

SERVES 4 TO 6

TOMATO, CREAM, AND VODKA SAUCE

POMODORO, PANNA E VODKA

This is another very good and quick sauce that uses a nice splash of vodka.

2 tablespoons unsalted butter

2 tablespoons extra virgin olive oil

¼ pound sliced pancetta, diced

⅓ cup vodka

1 (28-ounce) can whole Italian plum tomatoes, with juice and put through a food mill to remove seeds

⅓ cup heavy cream

Salt and freshly ground pepper, to taste

1 pound spaghetti

½ cup freshly grated Parmigiano-Reggiano cheese, divided

1 Heat the butter and oil in a large skillet over medium heat. Add the pancetta and stir until lightly colored. Lower the heat and carefully add the vodka. Stir until most of it has evaporated. Add the tomatoes and cream, season with salt and pepper, and simmer, uncovered, until sauce has a medium-thick consistency, 6 to 8 minutes.

2 Meanwhile, cook spaghetti in boiling salted water according to package directions.

3 Drain pasta and place in the skillet with the sauce. Add half of Parmigiano and mix over low heat until pasta and sauce are well combined. Taste, adjust the seasoning, and serve with a little more Parmigiano.

NOTE: Be careful when cooking with alcohol. Remove the skillet from the heat before adding the liquor. Carefully return the skillet back to the heat and gently stir over medium-low heat until the alcohol is almost all evaporated. Occasionally the alcohol will flame up. If that happens, turn off the heat and allow the alcohol to burn off or put the lid of another skillet over the flame to subdue it. Never throw water on the fire.

SERVES 4 TO 6

TOMATOES, PANCETTA, AND HOT PEPPER SAUCE ROMAN STYLE

POMODORO, PANCETTA E PEPERONCINO ALLA ROMANA

This is an amazing tasting and fast dish to prepare. Keep these ingredients on hand, and in 10 to 15 minutes, you will be sitting at your kitchen table savoring one of the best dishes that Rome has to offer.

⅓ cup extra virgin olive oil

4 ounces sliced smoked pancetta, diced

½ cup finely minced yellow onion

1 (28-ounce) can whole Italian plum tomatoes, with juice and put through a food mill to remove seeds

Salt and hot red pepper flakes, to taste

¼ cup fresh oregano leaves, shredded

1 pound spaghetti

½ cup freshly grated Parmigiano-Reggiano cheese

1 Heat the oil in a large skillet over medium heat. Add the pancetta and stir until it is lightly golden. Add the onion and keep stirring until it is pale yellow and soft, 4 to 5 minutes. Stir in the tomatoes and season with salt and red pepper flakes, and cook, uncovered, over medium heat until sauce begins to thicken, 8 to 10 minutes. Add the oregano to the sauce, stir once or twice, and turn off the heat.

2 Meanwhile, cook spaghetti in boiling salted water according to package directions.

3 Drain pasta and place in a warm serving bowl. Add about half of the sauce and a generous sprinkling of the cheese and quickly toss until pasta and sauce are well combined. Add a little more sauce and cheese, if needed, and serve at once.

SERVES 4 TO 6

TOMATOES, BUTTER, AND PARMIGIANO

POMODORO, BURRO E PARMIGIANO

This is one of the dishes I used to cook for my daughters, Carla and Paola, because it was very simple and very quick, especially when they came home from school and seemed to always be starving. If you have younger children, start them with this sauce, then slowly go on to more assertive ingredients.

5 tablespoons unsalted butter, divided

1 (28-ounce) can whole Italian plum tomatoes, with juice and put through a food mill to remove seeds

Salt, to taste

1 pound spaghetti

1 to 1½ cups grated Parmigiano-Reggiano cheese

1 Heat 3 tablespoons of butter in a medium saucepan. Add the tomatoes and bring to a simmer. Season with salt and cook, stirring until sauce has a medium-thick consistency, about 10 minutes.

2 Meanwhile, cook spaghetti in boiling salted water according to package directions.

3 Drain pasta and place in a large warm serving bowl. Add the remaining butter, sauce, and half of the Parmigiano. Mix until pasta, sauce, and cheese are well combined. Taste, adjust the seasoning, and top with a generous sprinkle of Parmigiano.

SERVES 4 TO 6

TOMATOES, CAPERS, AND OLIVES

POMODORO CON SUGO ALLA PUTTANESCA

This classic dish of Naples shows the creativity of the Neapolitans who are masters in preparing delicious dishes with only a few ingredients. Generally this type of sauce does not require cheese.

½ cup extra virgin olive oil

4 anchovy filets, chopped

2 cloves garlic, minced

1 tablespoon chopped fresh parsley

2 tablespoons capers, rinsed

1 cup black or green pitted olives, thinly sliced

1 (28-ounce) can whole Italian plum tomatoes, with juice and put through a food mill to remove seeds

Salt and freshly ground pepper, to taste

1 pound spaghetti

1 Heat the oil in a large skillet over medium heat. Add the anchovies, garlic, parsley, capers, and olives and stir for 1 to 2 minutes. Add the tomatoes, season with salt and pepper, and cook, stirring 8 to 10 minutes or until sauce has medium-thick consistency.

2 Meanwhile, cook spaghetti in boiling salted water according to package direction.

3 Drain spaghetti and add to the skillet. Quickly mix everything over low heat until the pasta and sauce are well combined. Taste, adjust the seasoning, and serve.

SERVES 4 TO 6

UNCOOKED SUMMER TOMATOES AND HERBS

SPAGHETTI CON POMODORO CRUDO

This is a great summer sauce because it can be made a few hours ahead of serving time. You can toss it with pasta or use as a side dish to grilled fish or meat. It can also become the topping of a bruschetta.

2 pounds fresh plum tomatoes, washed, seeded and diced

4 salt-packed plump white anchovy filets, rinsed and chopped, optional

½ cup pitted black olives, cut into quarters

½ cup finely minced shallots

2 to 3 cloves garlic, minced

½ cup mixed chopped fresh herbs (basil, oregano, marjoram, mint)

Salt and freshly ground pepper, to taste

½ cup extra virgin olive oil

1 pound spaghetti

½ cup grated Pecorino Romano cheese

1 Put the tomatoes in a strainer and place over a bowl for about 30 minutes to discard the watery juices.

2 Place the tomatoes, anchovies, olives, shallots, garlic, and fresh herbs into a large bowl that can later accommodate the pasta. Season with salt and pepper, add the oil, and mix well. Taste and adjust the seasoning. Cover the bowl and set aside.

3 Meanwhile, cook spaghetti in boiling salted water according to package directions.

4 Drain pasta and place in the bowl with the herbs and tomatoes. Quickly toss until pasta and sauce are well combined. Taste, adjust the seasoning, and serve with a sprinkle of cheese.

SERVES 4 TO 6

VEGETABLE

68 Baby Artichokes with Garlic, Capers, and Olives

69 Spring Vegetables, Smoked Ham, and Egg Sauce

70 Broccoli, Sausage, and Hot Pepper

71 Butternut Squash and Cream

72 Cauliflower with Olives and Capers

73 Eggplant, Anchovies, and Capers

74 Mushrooms, Prosciutto, and Cream

75 Olive Oil, Garlic, Oregano, and Hot Pepper

76 Peppers, Onion, Tomatoes, and Balsamic Sauce

78 Prosciutto, Tomatoes, and Peas

80 Roasted Cherry Tomatoes and Fava Beans

81 Roasted Vegetables with Balsamic Vinegar

82 Sautéed Mixed Mushrooms with Parsley and Sage

84 Zucchini, Onion, and Pancetta

BABY ARTICHOKES WITH GARLIC, CAPERS, AND OLIVES

CARCIOFINI MARINATI CON OLIO, AGLIO, CAPPERI E OLIVE

This is a dish for the long days of summer when the hot kitchen does not appeal to anyone. Prepare the artichokes ahead of time and put them together with all the other ingredients to marinate about one hour before serving. Cook the pasta and toss it with the room temperature ingredients.

3 pounds baby artichokes

½ cup extra virgin olive oil

2 cloves garlic, finely minced

⅓ cup capers, rinsed, patted dry, and roughly minced

⅓ cup roughly minced black olives

2 tablespoons minced Italian parsley

Salt and freshly ground pepper, to taste

1 pound spaghetti

1 Remove the outside leaves from the artichokes until you reach the pale tender leaves of the heart. Cut off the green tops and the green bottoms at the base and remove any green parts around the artichokes.

2 Drop the artichokes into boiling water and cook, uncovered, over medium heat until the bottom of artichokes can easily be pierced with a knife, 4 to 5 minutes depending on size. Drain and place in a bowl of iced water to cool. Drain again and pat dry with paper towels. Cut artichokes into thin slices and set aside.

3 In a large bowl that can later accommodate the pasta, combine olive oil, garlic, capers, olives, and parsley and season with salt and a generous amount of pepper. Add the artichoke hearts and stir to incorporate.

4 Meanwhile, cook spaghetti in boiling salted water according to package directions.

5 Drain spaghetti and place in the bowl. Quickly mix everything until pasta and sauce are well combined. Taste, adjust the seasoning, and serve.

SERVES 4 TO 6

SPRING VEGETABLES, SMOKED HAM, AND EGG SAUCE

SPAGHETTI CON SPECK, PISELLI, ASPARAGI, FAVE E UOVA

When my daughters were fairly young, they were not fond of vegetables. But if I tossed the vegetables with a creamy egg and Parmigiano mixture, they finished everything on their plate. Today, I still use the same technique with my grandchildren.

1 cup shelled fresh or frozen peas, thawed if frozen

1 cup shelled fresh or frozen fava beans, thawed if frozen

1 cup fresh or frozen asparagus tips, thawed if frozen

4 egg yolks

2 large eggs

1 cup freshly grated Parmigiano-Reggiano cheese, divided

Salt and freshly ground pepper, to taste

1 pound spaghetti

½ cup extra virgin olive oil

6 ounces thinly sliced smoked ham cut into 1-inch pieces

1 If you are using fresh vegetables, cook them separately in salted boiling water until tender, 2 to 4 minutes depending on size. Drain and set aside.

2 In a large serving bowl that can later accommodate the pasta, beat the egg yolks, eggs, and about half of the Parmigiano and stir until well combined. Season with salt and a generous amount of pepper. Set aside.

3 Meanwhile, cook spaghetti in boiling salted water according to package directions.

4 While the pasta is cooking, heat the oil in a large skillet over medium heat. Add the ham and stir for a minute or two. Add all the vegetables, season lightly with salt, and stir until they are heated through.

5 Drain pasta and place in the bowl with the eggs. Add the ham and the vegetables and quickly mix until pasta is well coated with the sauce. Taste, adjust the seasoning, and serve with additional Parmigiano.

SERVES 4 TO 6

BROCCOLI, SAUSAGE, AND HOT PEPPER

SALSICCIA, BROCCOLI E PEPERONCINO

This is a dish typical of southern Italy which combines sweet sausage, broccoli florets, and great olive oil into a most appetizing dish.

3 cups broccoli florets, fresh or frozen

1 pound spaghetti

½ cup extra virgin olive oil

½ pound sweet Italian sausage, casing removed

2 cloves garlic, minced

½ to 1 cup vegetable broth

2 tablespoons unsalted butter

Salt and hot red pepper flakes, to taste

1 Boil broccoli florets in salted water until tender but still a bit firm to the bite, 2 to 3 minutes. Drain, dry with paper towels, and roughly chop into very small pieces.

2 Meanwhile, cook spaghetti in boiling salted water according to package directions.

3 While pasta cooks, heat oil in a large skillet over medium-high heat. Mince the sausage, add to the skillet, and stir until lightly golden, 3 to 4 minutes. Add the broccoli, garlic, broth, and butter. Season with salt and red pepper flakes and stir well to combine.

4 Drain pasta, add to the skillet, and stir until pasta and vegetables are well combined. Taste, adjust the seasoning, and add a little more oil if needed. Serve at once.

SERVE 4 TO 6

BUTTERNUT SQUASH AND CREAM

SUGO DI ZUCCA E PANNA

This is a great fall and winter dish that will fill you as well as satisfy you.

1 medium butternut squash, about 1 pound

4 tablespoons unsalted butter

½ cup finely minced shallots

1½ cup heavy cream

1 cup chicken broth, divided

Salt, to taste

1 tablespoon chopped fresh flat-leaf parsley

1 pound spaghetti

½ cup freshly grated Parmigiano-Reggiano cheese

1 Preheat oven to 400 F. Peel, cut squash in half lengthwise, remove seeds, and cut it into 1-inch pieces. Place squash on an oiled baking sheet and roast until golden and soft, about 15 minutes.

2 Heat the butter in a large skillet over medium heat. Add the shallots and stir for 2 to 3 minutes. Add the cream and ½ cup of the broth, season with salt, and simmer until sauce begins to thicken, about 2 to 3 minutes. Add the squash and parsley; stir for a minute or two. Taste and adjust the seasoning and turn off the heat.

3 Meanwhile, cook spaghetti in boiling salted water according to package directions.

4 Drain spaghetti and add to a large warm serving bowl. Add a nice handful of Parmigiano and toss well to combine. Add a little bit of broth if sauce seems too thick. Taste, adjust the seasoning, and serve with a little more Parmigiano.

SERVES 4 TO 6

CAULIFLOWER WITH OLIVES AND CAPERS

CAVOLFIORE CON OLIVE E CAPPERI

One of my favorite stress-free pasta dishes is "spaghetti Aglio e Olio," a dish that my mother-in-law, who came from Salerno, use to prepare weekly. This dish is the base of several other similar preparations, just like this one which I added cauliflower florets, capers, and olives.

1 large cauliflower
1 pound spaghetti
⅓ to ½ cup extra virgin olive oil
2 cloves garlic, minced
1 tablespoon minced parsley
2 tablespoons capers, rinsed
8 pitted black olives, thinly sliced
Salt and hot red pepper flakes, to taste

1 Cut the cauliflower into florets, discarding the core, and boil in salted water until very tender, 4 to 5 minutes. Drain, dry with paper towels, and chop the florets into small pieces. Set aside.

2 Meanwhile, cook spaghetti in boiling salted water according to package directions.

3 While the pasta cooks, heat the oil in a large skillet over medium heat. Add the garlic, parsley, capers, and olives; season with salt and red pepper flakes and stir for a minute or two. Stir in the cauliflower and mix it with the sauce until well combined.

4 Drain pasta, add to the skillet, and stir until pasta and sauce are well combined. Taste and adjust the seasoning and add a little more oil if needed.

SERVES 4 TO 6

EGGPLANT, ANCHOVIES, AND CAPERS

MELANZANE AL FUNGHETTO

The word "funghetto" is a combination of appetizing ingredients such as eggplant, mushrooms, anchovies, capers, olives, and herbs that are cooked together. This mixture is kept together and unified by a fruitful olive oil. I love it over pasta, just as in this recipe, or as a topping for grilled bread.

3 medium-size firm eggplants

Salt

½ cup extra virgin olive oil

2 cloves garlic, minced

4 oil-packed anchovies, drained and minced

⅓ cup capers, rinsed and minced

2 tablespoons chopped fresh parsley

Salt and freshly ground pepper, to taste

1 pound spaghetti

1 Peel and dice the eggplant into ½-inch cubes. Place the eggplant in a large colander, sprinkle with salt, and let stand for 15 to 20 minutes. (The salt will release the bitter juices). Pat the eggplant dry with paper towels.

2 Heat the oil in a large skillet. Add the eggplant, without crowding, and cook over medium-high heat until lightly golden. Add the garlic, anchovies, and capers and stir for about 1 minute. Add the parsley and season with salt and pepper. Taste, adjust the seasoning, and turn off the heat.

3 Meanwhile, cook spaghetti in boiling salted water according to package directions.

4 Drain spaghetti and add to the skillet. Quickly mix everything over low heat until pasta and eggplant are well combined. Taste, adjust the seasoning, and serve.

SERVES 4 TO 6

MUSHROOMS, PROSCIUTTO, AND CREAM

FUNGHI, PROSCIUTTO E PANNA

This dish is delicious and goes together quickly. Make sure, however, not to reduce the cream too much. If that should happen, turn off the heat, scoop up about ½ cup of the pasta cooking water, and add it to the sauce and then stir and serve.

1 pound spaghetti

3 tablespoons unsalted butter

2 tablespoons extra virgin olive oil

1½ pounds fresh mixed mushrooms, wiped clean and cut into thin slices

2 cloves garlic, minced

2 tablespoons chopped parsley

5 ounces sliced prosciutto, diced

1½ cups heavy cream

Salt and freshly ground pepper, to taste

½ cup freshly grated Parmigiano-Reggiano cheese

1 Cook spaghetti in boiling salted water according to package directions.

2 Meanwhile, heat the butter and oil in a large skillet. When the butter foams, add the mushrooms, without crowding the skillet, and sauté over high heat until golden, 3 to 4 minutes. Reduce the heat to medium, add the garlic, parsley, and prosciutto and stir for 1 to 2 minutes. Add the cream and season with salt and pepper. Simmer gently for 3 to 4 minutes until the cream is reduced almost by half. Stir in ½ cup of the pasta cooking water if needed.

3 Drain spaghetti and add to the skillet. Mix over low heat until pasta and sauce are well combined. Serve with a sprinkle of Parmigiano.

SERVE 4 TO 6

OLIVE OIL, GARLIC, OREGANO, AND HOT PEPPER

OLIO, AGLIO, OREGANO E PEPERONCINO

One of the most appreciated Tuscan peasant dishes is made with a wonderful extra virgin olive oil, a sprinkle of salt, lots of black pepper, and country bread. The bread is dipped into the oil mixture. In Naples, and in many parts of the southern Italian regions, they take the same sauce and toss it with spaghetti! This is a terrific dish that costs you almost nothing and it is made in the spur of the moment.

1 pound spaghetti
½ cup extra virgin olive oil
3 cloves garlic, thinly minced
1 to 2 teaspoons hot red pepper flakes
Salt, to taste
2 tablespoons minced fresh oregano
2 tablespoons minced parsley

1 Cook spaghetti in boiling salt water according to package directions.

2 Meanwhile, heat the oil in a large skillet over medium heat. Add the garlic and red pepper flakes and season with salt. When the garlic just begins to color, add the oregano and the parsley, stir once or twice, and turn off the heat.

3 Drain spaghetti and add to the skillet. Mix everything quickly over low heat until pasta is well coated with the aromatic oil. Taste, adjust the seasoning, and serve.

SERVES 4 TO 6

PEPPERS, ONION, TOMATOES, AND BALSAMIC SAUCE

PEPERONATA IN PADELLA

When I make this delicious dish, I use half of the vegetable sauce tossed with pasta, and the other half, I save for the next night for a peppery grilled steak.

½ cup extra virgin olive oil

4 large red, yellow, and green bell peppers, seeded and cut into ½-inch thin strips

2 large onions, thinly sliced

4 large fresh tomatoes, seeded and cut into small chunks

Salt and freshly ground pepper, to taste

3 tablespoons good quality imported Balsamic vinegar

1 pound spaghetti

1 Heat the oil in a large skillet over medium heat. Add the peppers and cook, stirring, until the skin begins to color, 4 to 5 minutes.

2 Add the onion and stir until it just begins to soften, 5 to 6 minutes. Add the tomatoes and cook until they begin to soften, 3 to 4 minutes. Season with salt and pepper and a drizzle of the vinegar.

3 Reduce the heat to medium low and cook, stirring occasionally, until vegetables are tender and their juices have thickened, 4 to 5 minutes. (This sauce can be prepared several hours ahead and gently reheated.)

4 Meanwhile, cook spaghetti in boiling salted water according to package directions.

5 Drain and add pasta to a large serving bowl. Add half of the sauce and mix well to combine. Taste, adjust the seasoning, and serve.

SERVES 4 TO 6

PROSCIUTTO, TOMATOES, AND PEAS

PROSCIUTTO, POMODORO E PISELLI

Ripe tomatoes, spring shallots, peas, and prosciutto are all ingredients used in this dish. I love the clean sweet flavor that enriches this simple quick sauce.

1 ½ pounds unshelled fresh peas or 1 (10-ounce) package frozen peas, thawed

½ cup extra virgin olive oil

½ cup minced shallots

2 cloves garlic, minced

5 to 6 fresh plum tomatoes, minced

Salt and freshly ground pepper, to taste

¼ pound sliced prosciutto, diced

1 pound spaghetti

2 tablespoons unsalted butter

½ cup freshly grated Parmigiano-Reggiano cheese

1 Shell the fresh peas and cook them in a medium saucepan of boiling salted water until tender but still firm to the bite, 3 to 4 minutes. Drain and set aside.

2 Heat the oil in a large skillet over medium heat. Add the shallots and cook until lightly golden and soft. Add the garlic, stir once or twice, and then add the tomatoes. Season with salt and pepper and cook until tomatoes begin to soften, 4 to 5 minutes. Add the prosciutto, stir for a minute or two, and then add the peas. Stir until peas are heated through. Turn off the heat.

3 Meanwhile, cook spaghetti in boiling salted water according to package directions.

4 When pasta is almost done, scoop up and reserve ½ cup of the cooking water. Drain spaghetti and add to the skillet. Add the butter and mix quickly over low heat until pasta and sauce are well combined. Add a little of the reserved cooking water if needed. Taste, adjust the seasoning, and serve with a little sprinkle of Parmigiano.

SERVES 4 TO 6

ROASTED CHERRY TOMATOES AND FAVA BEANS

POMODORINI AL FORNO CON FAVE

If you cook with seasonal produce, you will save money and enjoy the most flavorful ingredients.

1½ pounds cherry tomatoes, cut in halves

Salt and freshly ground pepper, to taste

½ cup olive oil, divided

2 pounds fresh fava beans or fresh peas in their pods

½ cup minced shallots

2 cloves garlic, minced

1 pound spaghetti

1 Preheat oven to 300 F. Line a baking sheet with parchment paper. Place the cherry tomatoes in a medium bowl, season with salt and pepper, and toss with a few tablespoons of the olive oil. Spread the tomatoes all over the paper and roast until they begin to shrivel, 15 to 20 minutes. Remove tomatoes, place in a bowl, and set aside.

2 If fava beans are young and fresh, there is no need to peel them. If not, blanch them in a pot of salted water for less than one minute. Drain and chill under cold running water. Pinch the skin of each bean and squeeze out the bean. Set aside. (Tomatoes and beans can be precooked a few hours ahead.)

3 Heat the remaining oil in a large skillet over medium heat. Add the shallots and cook over low heat until lightly golden, 3 to 4 minutes. Add the garlic and stir for about 1 minute. Add the roasted tomatoes and the fava beans and season with salt and pepper. Stir for 2 to 3 minutes or until the vegetables are nice and hot, then turn off the heat.

4 Meanwhile, cook spaghetti in boiling, salted water according to package instructions.

5 Drain spaghetti and add to the skillet. Quickly mix everything over low heat until pasta and sauce are well combined. Taste, adjust the seasoning, and serve.

SERVES 4 TO 6

ROASTED VEGETABLES WITH BALSAMIC VINEGAR

VERDURE ARROSTO CON BALSAMICO

I love to roast vegetables because I can serve them as a side dish, stirred into a risotto, or as a sauce with pasta. Double the amount of vegetables and save for the next day—perhaps tossed with another pasta or scrambled with a few eggs.

3 medium red bell peppers, cored, seeded, and cut into 1-inch pieces

Salt and freshly ground pepper, to taste

1 cup extra virgin olive oil, divided

3 medium zucchini, trimmed and cut into 1-inch pieces

3 small eggplant, trimmed and cut into 1-inch pieces

1 pound spaghetti

2 tablespoons Balsamic vinegar

4 to 6 basil leaves, shredded

1 Preheat oven to 375 F. Place peppers in a large bowl, season generously with salt, pepper, and about half of the olive oil. Stir well and spread on a baking sheet with sides.

2 Put the zucchini and eggplant into the same large bowl, season with salt, pepper, and the remaining olive oil and spread on another baking sheet with sides. Place all the vegetables into the hot oven and stir once or twice until they have a golden brown color. About 20 minutes for the peppers and 15 minutes for the zucchini and eggplant.

3 Meanwhile, cook spaghetti in boiling salted water according to package direction.

4 While the pasta cooks, place the roasted vegetables into a large warm bowl. Add the vinegar and basil and stir to combine.

5 Drain pasta, add to the bowl, and toss until pasta and vegetables are well combined. Taste, adjust the seasoning, and serve.

SERVES 4 TO 6

SAUTÉED MIXED MUSHROOMS WITH PARSLEY AND SAGE

FUNGHI ALLA BOSCAIOLA

If you like mushrooms, you will fall in love with this dish. Choose a variety of mixed mushrooms, (shiitake, porcini, oyster, and chanterelle), cook over high heat until golden, add the garlic and the herbs, season with salt and pepper, and the sauce is done. Buon Appetito!

½ cup extra virgin olive oil

1 pound mixed mushrooms, wiped clean and thinly sliced

2 cloves garlic, minced

Salt and freshly ground pepper, to taste

1 pound spaghetti

1 tablespoon unsalted butter

3 tablespoons minced parsley

1 tablespoon minced sage

1 Heat the oil in a large skillet over high heat. Add the mushrooms and cook, stirring, until they are golden, 4 to 5 minutes. Add the garlic, season with salt and pepper, and stir a few times. Taste and adjust the seasoning and turn off the heat.

2 Meanwhile, cook spaghetti in boiling salted water according to package directions.

3 Drain spaghetti and add to the skillet. Add butter, parsley, and sage and quickly mix everything over low heat until the pasta and mushrooms are well combined. Taste, adjust the seasoning, and serve.

SERVES 4 TO 6

ZUCCHINI, ONION, AND PANCETTA

ZUCCHINI, CIPOLLE E PANCETTA

The amazing onion! When this vegetable is cooked very slowly for a length of time, it becomes very soft, tender, and delicious. The addition of zucchini and pancetta adds additional flavor.

½ to ¾ cup extra virgin olive oil

4 small zucchini cut into small cubes

½ cup water

5 cups thinly sliced yellow onion

6 ounces thinly sliced pancetta, cut into 1-inch pieces

Salt and freshly ground pepper, to taste

1 pound spaghetti

1 Heat the oil in a large skillet. Add the zucchini and cook over medium heat until lightly golden 4 to 5 minutes. Scoop up the zucchini with a slotted spoon and place in a bowl. Set aside.

2 Add a little more oil in the skillet if needed, stir in water and onions and cover the skillet. Simmer over low heat for 15 to 20 minutes, stirring a few times, until onion is pale yellow and very soft. Add a little more water if needed.

3 Remove the lid and raise the heat. Add the pancetta and stir until the pancetta and the onion take on a light golden color. Add the zucchini, season with salt and pepper, and toss a few times.

4 Meanwhile, cook spaghetti in boiling salted water according to package directions.

5 Drain spaghetti and add to the skillet. Quickly mix everything over low heat until the vegetables and pasta are well combined. Taste, adjust the seasoning, and serve.

SERVES 4 TO 6

SEAFOOD

88 Anchovies, Bread Crumbs, Pine Nuts, and Raisins

89 Bottarga, Sun-Dried Tomatoes, and Virgin Olive Oil

90 Clams with White Wine and Hot Pepper

92 Lobster and Summer Tomatoes

94 Swordfish, Eggplant, and Sun-Dried Tomatoes

95 Monkfish with Olives and Tomatoes

96 Mussels, Saffron, and Cherry Tomatoes

97 Prawns with Broccoli Florets and Paprika

98 Scallops, Cherry Tomatoes, and Hot Pepper

99 Shrimp, Garlic, Vodka, Tomatoes, and Cream

100 Smoked Salmon, Shallots, Cream, and Lemon Zest

102 Spicy Tuna and Tomato Sauce

103 Squid, Tomatoes, and Mint

104 Squid with Broccoli Rabe

ANCHOVIES, BREAD CRUMBS, PINE NUTS, AND RAISINS

ACCIUGHE CON MOLLICA DI PANE, PIGNOLI E UVETTA

In the old peasant tradition, fried bread crumbs were used instead of more expensive cheese to coat the pasta with a delightful crispness.

4 ounces of pane pugliese or baguette, cut into medium chunks

¾ cup extra virgin olive oil, divided

4 to 5 oil-packed anchovy filets, chopped

3 cloves garlic, minced

½ cup pine nuts, lightly toasted

½ cup raisins, soaked in lukewarm water until soft and drained

Salt and hot red pepper flakes, to taste

1 pound spaghetti

2 tablespoons minced fresh parsley

1 Preheat oven to 325 F. Place the bread in a bowl, toss with about ¼ cup of the oil, and spread on a baking sheet. Bake until the bread is lightly golden outside but a little soft inside, 8 to 10 minutes. Cool the bread, place it in the bowl of a food processor, and pulse on and off until it becomes fine crumbs. Set aside. Makes approximately ¾ cup bread crumbs.

2 Heat the remaining oil in a large skillet over medium heat. Add the anchovies, garlic, pine nuts, and raisins; season with salt and red pepper flakes and stir for 1 to 2 minutes. Turn off the heat.

3 Meanwhile, cook spaghetti in boiling salted water according to package directions.

4 Drain pasta and place in the skillet with the sauce. Add the parsley and toss everything over low heat until well combined. Just before you are ready to place spaghetti on plates, taste and adjust the seasoning, and sprinkle the bread crumbs over each serving.

SERVES 4 TO 6

BOTTARGA, SUN-DRIED TOMATOES, AND VIRGIN OLIVE OIL

BOTTARGA E POMODORI SECCHI

Bottarga, made from the dried, salted, pressed roe of gray mullet or tuna, is traditionally preserved and appreciated on the islands of Sicily and Sardinia. If you can get bottarga imported from Southern Italy, get it. Make a simple sauce of garlic and olive oil then grate or shave the bottarga over the spaghetti and enjoy the lively flavors.

½ cup extra virgin olive oil

2 cloves garlic, roughly minced

½ cup minced sun-dried tomatoes

1 tablespoon hot red pepper flakes

2 tablespoons minced Italian parsley

1 pound spaghetti

1 (2-ounce) piece bottarga, grey mullet or tuna

1 Heat the oil in a large skillet over medium heat. Add the garlic, tomatoes, and red pepper flakes and stir for about 2 minutes. Add the parsley, stir, and turn off the heat.

2 Meanwhile, cook spaghetti in boiling salted water according to package directions.

3 When the pasta is almost done, scoop up and reserve ½ cup of the pasta cooking water. Drain pasta, place in the skillet with the sauce, and toss well over low heat. Add a little of the reserved cooking water if it seems too dry.

4 Transfer the pasta to a warm large bowl, grate some of the bottarga over the pasta, and toss. Serve with a little more bottarga, if you wish.

SERVES 4 TO 6

CLAMS WITH WHITE WINE AND HOT PEPPER

VONGOLE, VINO BIANCO E PEPERONCINO

Italians are in love with simple, straight forward rustic dishes. Perhaps the reason is that they are quick to prepare, pleasing to the eye, and very, very good.

2 ½ pounds small littleneck or manila clams

1 cup water

½ cup extra virgin olive oil, divided

2 cloves garlic, minced

1 cup good quality white wine

Salt and hot red pepper flakes, to taste

1 pound spaghetti

2 tablespoons finely chopped flat-leaf parsley

1 to 2 tablespoons unsalted butter, optional

1 Soak the clams in a bowl of cold water for 20 to 30 minutes to purge them. Wash and scrub them under cold running water and place in a large skillet. Add water and 2 tablespoons oil. Cover the skillet and cook until clams open, about 1 minute. Toss out any clams that do not open. Detach the clam meat from the shell and place in a bowl. Line a small strainer with paper towels and strain the clam juices from the skillet into a separate bowl. Set juice aside.

2 Wipe the skillet clean with paper towels, add the remaining olive oil, and warm over medium heat. Add the garlic and stir until pale yellow. Add the wine and the reserved clam juice, season with salt and red pepper flakes, and stir until the juices begin to thicken, 2 to 3 minutes. Add the clams, stir once or twice until clams are coated with the savory sauce, and turn off the heat.

3 Meanwhile, cook spaghetti in boiling salted water according to package direction.

4 When pasta is almost done, scoop up and reserve about ½ cup of the cooking water. Drain spaghetti and add to the skillet. Add the parsley and butter, if using, taste, and adjust the seasoning. Toss over low heat until pasta and sauce are well combined. Add some of the reserved cooking water if pasta looks a bit dry. Taste and adjust the seasoning and serve at once.

SERVES 4 TO 6

LOBSTER AND SUMMER TOMATOES

ARAGOSTA E POMODORO FRESCHI

In this dish, sweet summer tomatoes are paired with chunks of lobster tail and briefly cooked. Fresh basil leaves are added and tossed with the spaghetti. This is a delicious sauce that can be put together in less than 15 minutes!

½ cup extra virgin olive oil

2 cloves garlic

2 (9 ounces each) fresh or frozen lobster tails, shelled and cut into ½-inch pieces

2 tablespoons minced sun-dried tomatoes

2 pounds fresh tomatoes, seeded and diced

Salt and pepper, to taste

A few leaves fresh basil, shredded

2 tablespoons unsalted butter

1 pound spaghetti

1 Heat the oil in a large skillet over medium heat. Add the garlic and when golden brown, discard. Add the lobster pieces and cook, stirring until lobster just begins to color, 1 to 2 minutes. Add the tomatoes, season with salt and pepper, and stir for 2 to 3 minutes. Stir in the basil and butter then turn the heat off under the skillet.

2 Meanwhile, cook spaghetti in boiling salted water according to package directions.

3 Drain pasta and add to the skillet. Quickly toss to combine with the sauce. Taste, adjust the seasoning, and serve.

SERVES 4 TO 6

SWORDFISH, EGGPLANT, AND SUN-DRIED TOMATOES

PESCE SPADA, MELANZANE E POMODORI SECCHI

The Southern Italian diet is possibly the best in Italy. Seafood, vegetables, extra virgin olive oil, and a variety of herbs give a terrific flavor to the food of the various areas. The pasta in Southern Italy is quick, delicious and very healthy.

1 medium eggplant

Salt

½ cup extra virgin olive oil

½ cup finely minced yellow onion

2 cloves garlic, minced

¾ pound swordfish steak, cut into ½-inch cubes

2 tablespoons capers, rinsed, dried, and minced

½ cup minced black olives

⅓ cup roughly chopped sun-dried tomatoes

Freshly ground pepper, to taste

1 pound spaghetti

1 Trim and peel the eggplant and cut into ⅓-inch-thick rounds. Place the slices on a large baking sheet, sprinkle liberally with salt, and let stand 30 to 40 minutes to allow the bitter juices of the eggplant to come to the surface. Pat the slices well with paper towels and cut the eggplant into ⅓-inch cubes.

2 Heat the oil in a large skillet over medium-high heat. Add the eggplant and stir until it has a nice golden color. Transfer to paper towels to drain.

3 Discard some of the oil, if needed, and then add the onion and garlic and cook, stirring over medium heat, until soft and lightly golden, 4 to 5 minutes. Add the swordfish and stir for a minute or two or until it begins to color. Add the capers, olives, and tomatoes, stir for about 2 minutes, and then add the eggplant. Season with pepper and turn off the heat under the skillet. Add a little more oil, if needed.

4 Meanwhile, cook spaghetti in boiling salted water according to package directions.

5 Drain spaghetti and place in the skillet. Toss everything well over low heat, taste and adjust the seasoning, and serve.

SERVES 4 TO 6

MONKFISH WITH OLIVES AND TOMATOES

RANA PESCATRICE, OLIVE E POMODORO

If your pantry is well stocked, you can whip up this sauce in no time at all. Instead of monkfish, you can use any fish or shellfish of your liking, or you can omit the fish all together.

½ cup extra virgin olive oil

1 pound monkfish, washed, patted dry, and cut into ½-inch cubes

Salt and freshly ground pepper, to taste

4 oil-packed anchovy filets, minced, optional

2 cloves garlic, minced

3 tablespoons minced black olives

1 cup dry white wine

1 (28-ounce) can Italian plum tomatoes, with juice and put through a food mill to remove seeds

2 tablespoons chopped fresh parsley

1 pound spaghetti

1 Heat the oil in a large skillet over medium heat. Season the fish with salt and pepper and add to the hot oil without crowding. Cook, turning once, until the fish has a nice golden color, 2 to 3 minutes. Transfer to a plate.

2 Add the anchovies, garlic, and olives and stir for about 1 minute. Add the wine and stir, scraping the bottom of the skillet with a wooden spoon, until wine is almost all reduced. Add the tomatoes and bring the sauce to a simmer. Cook, stirring from time to time, until sauce has medium-thick consistency, 6 to 7 minutes.

3 Return the monkfish to the skillet, add the parsley, and simmer the sauce for 1 to 2 minutes. Taste and adjust the seasoning.

4 Meanwhile, cook spaghetti in boiling salted water according to package directions.

5 Drain pasta and place in a warm serving bowl. Add about half of the sauce and quickly toss to combine. Add more sauce, if needed. Taste, adjust the seasoning, and serve.

SERVES 4 TO 6

MUSSELS, SAFFRON, AND CHERRY TOMATOES

COZZE CON ZAFFERANO E POMODORINI

Mussels, saffron, and cherry tomatoes make this dish visually appealing. The saffron adds a rich color and the red pepper lifts the mood. The barely-cooked cherry tomatoes and the mussels tie everything together.

½ cup extra virgin olive oil, divided

3 pounds mussels

1 pinch of saffron

½ cup finely minced shallots

2 cloves garlic, minced

1 pound ripe cherry tomatoes, washed and halved

1 tablespoon chopped flat-leaf parsley

1 tablespoon unsalted butter

Salt and hot red pepper flakes, to taste

1 pound spaghetti

1 Heat half of the oil in a large skillet over medium heat. Add the mussels, cover the skillet, and cook until mussels open, 2 to 4 minutes. Transfer them to a bowl as they open, discard the ones that don't open, and detach the mussel meat from the shells. Discard the shells. Line a small strainer with a cheese cloth and strain the mussel juices from the skillet into a separate bowl. Add the saffron, stir well, and set aside.

2 Wipe the skillet clean with paper towels and place on medium heat. Add the remaining oil, shallots, and garlic and stir until they are lightly golden and soft. Add the tomatoes and cook until they begin to shrivel, 3 to 4 minutes. Add the reserved mussel juice and stir until it is reduced by half. Add the parsley, butter, and season with salt and red pepper flakes. Turn off the heat.

3 Meanwhile, cook spaghetti in boiling salted water according to package directions.

4 Drain the pasta and add to the skillet. Toss over low heat until pasta and sauce are well combined. Taste, adjust the seasoning, and serve.

SERVES 4 TO 6

PRAWNS WITH BROCCOLI FLORETS AND PAPRIKA

GAMBERI CON CIME DI BROCCOLI E PAPRIKA

There was a time when I used to eat a basic three course meal. Today, now that I am older, this is what I crave. Spaghetti with vegetables and seafood tossed with extra virgin olive oil, just a little butter, and hot pepper. And my dessert? Well, that is another story.

1 pound broccoli

⅓ cup extra virgin olive oil

2 tablespoons unsalted butter

½ cup finely minced onion

2 cloves garlic, minced

1 pound prawns, shelled and cut into 1-inch thick pieces

Salt and paprika, to taste

1 pound spaghetti

1 Detach the broccoli florets from the stems and set the stems aside for another use.

2 Bring a medium pot of salted water to a boil, add the broccoli florets, and cook until tender, 3 to 4 minutes. Scoop up the florets and transfer to a bowl of iced water to cool. Drain, pat dry, and cut the larger florets into smaller pieces.

3 Heat the oil and butter in a large skillet over medium heat. Add the onion and cook until lightly golden and soft. Add the garlic, stir once or twice, and then add the prawns. Season with salt and paprika and cook, stirring until prawns have a nice golden color, 1 to 2 minutes. Add broccoli to the skillet and stir over medium heat until the mixture is heated through. Taste and adjust the seasoning.

4 Meanwhile, cook spaghetti in boiling salted water according to package directions.

5 Drain pasta and place in a warm serving bowl. Add the sauce and quickly toss to combine. Taste, adjust the seasoning, and sprinkle with a little olive oil, if needed. Serve at once.

SERVES 4 TO 6

SCALLOPS, CHERRY TOMATOES, AND HOT PEPPER

CAPPE SANTE, POMODORINI E PEPERONCINO

This is the type of food that I like to cook on my day off; fresh, fast, and simple. The problem is that this dish is so delicious; I always succumb to another helping.

½ cup extra virgin olive oil

1 pound medium-size scallops, halved

1 pound cherry tomatoes, halved

1 tablespoon chopped flat-leaf parsley

2 cloves garlic, minced

Chopped fresh chile pepper or hot red pepper flakes, to taste

Salt, to taste

1 pound spaghetti

1 Heat the oil in a large skillet over high heat. When the oil is hot, add the scallops and stir until they have a golden color, 2 to 3 minutes. With a slotted spoon, transfer scallops to a serving bowl.

2 Put the skillet back on high heat, add the tomatoes and stir for 2 to 3 minutes until tomatoes begin to shrivel. Add parsley, garlic, and chile pepper and season lightly with salt. Stir for about 1 minute. Add the scallops and stir just long enough to heat them through.

3 Meanwhile, cook spaghetti in boiling salted water according to package directions.

4 Drain pasta and place in the serving bowl. Add the sauce and quickly toss to combine. Taste, adjust the seasoning, and serve.

SERVES 4 TO 6

SHRIMP, GARLIC, VODKA, TOMATOES, AND CREAM

GAMBERI CON AGLIO, VODKA, POMODORO E PANNA

*The simple **addition** of a small amount of cream will thicken up the sauce, add additional taste, and create an elegant color.*

⅓ cup extra virgin olive oil

2 tablespoons unsalted butter

1 pound large shrimp, cut into ½-inch pieces

3 cloves garlic

⅓ cup vodka

4 cups canned Italian plum tomatoes, with juice and put through a food mill to remove seeds

Salt and hot red pepper flakes, to taste

⅓ cup heavy cream

1 to 2 tablespoons chopped parsley

1 pound spaghetti

1 Heat the oil and butter in a large skillet over medium heat. Add the shrimp and cook until they are lightly golden, about 1 minute. Add the garlic, stir until it is golden brown, and then discard it. Carefully add the vodka and stir over low heat until vodka is almost all reduced. With a slotted spoon, transfer shrimp to a bowl while you finish the sauce.

2 Add the tomatoes, salt, and red pepper flakes. Cook, uncovered, over low heat, stirring occasionally for 8 to 10 minutes. Add the shrimp and parsley and stir for about 1 minute until shrimp and sauce are well combined.

3 Meanwhile, cook spaghetti in boiling salted water according to package directions.

4 Drain the pasta and place in the skillet with the sauce. Toss well and serve.

NOTE: Be careful when cooking with alcohol. Remove the skillet from the heat before adding the liquor. Carefully return the skillet back to the heat and gently stir over medium-low heat until the alcohol is almost all evaporated. Occasionally the alcohol will flame up. If that happens, turn off the heat and allow the alcohol to burn off or put the lid of another skillet over the flame to subdue it. Never throw water on the fire.

SERVES 4 TO 6

SMOKED SALMON, SHALLOTS, CREAM, AND LEMON ZEST

SALMONE AFFUMICATO SCALOGNO, PANNA E SCORZA DI LIMONE

A few ounces of smoked salmon are used in conjunction with minced shallots, cream, and lemon zest and turned into a mouthwatering sauce for pasta.

4 tablespoons unsalted butter

2 to 3 tablespoons finely chopped shallots

2 cloves garlic, minced

1 cup dry white wine

1½ cups heavy cream

Salt and white pepper, to taste

4 to 5 ounces smoked salmon, cut into small strips

Grated zest of 1 small lemon

2 tablespoons parsley

1 pound spaghetti

1 Heat the butter in a large skillet over medium heat. Add the shallots and garlic and stir constantly until shallots and garlic are lightly golden and soft, 3 to 4 minutes. Add the wine and stir until it is reduced approximately by half. Add the cream, season lightly with salt and pepper, and stir until it just begins to thicken, about 2 minutes. Add the salmon, lemon zest, and parsley. Stir less than 1 minute and turn off the heat.

2 Meanwhile, cook spaghetti in boiling salted water according to package directions.

3 When pasta is almost done, scoop up and reserve ½ cup of the cooking water. Drain the pasta and add to the skillet. Quickly mix over low heat until pasta and sauce are well combined. Add a little of the reserved cooking water, if needed. Taste, adjust the seasoning, and serve.

SERVES 4 TO 6

SPICY TUNA AND TOMATO SAUCE

INTINGOLO DI TONNO PICCANTE E POMODORO

In my pantry, I always have oil-packed tuna, canned tomatoes from Italy, capers, olives, and spaghetti. With these simple ingredients I can whip up a great spaghetti dish in no time at all.

1 (7-ounce) can oil-packed white tuna, preferably imported from Italy

⅓ cup extra virgin olive oil

1 clove garlic, minced

2 to 3 oil-packed anchovy filets, drained and minced

2 tablespoons capers, rinsed and minced

¼ cup minced black olives

3 to 4 cups canned Italian plum tomatoes, with juice and put through a food mill to remove seeds

Salt and hot red pepper flakes, to taste

1 pound spaghetti

1 Drain the tuna, place on a cutting board, and roughly chop.

2 Heat the oil in a medium saucepan over medium heat. Add the garlic and anchovies and stir until garlic just begins to color, 1 to 2 minutes. Add the tuna, capers, and olives and stir for about 2 minutes. Stir in the tomatoes, season with salt and red pepper flakes, and bring the sauce to a simmer. Cook over medium heat, uncovered, stirring from time to time until sauce has a medium-thick consistency, 8 to 10 minutes.

3 Meanwhile, cook spaghetti in boiling salted water according to package directions.

4 Drain pasta and place in a warm serving bowl. Add about half of the sauce and quickly toss to combine. Add a little more sauce, if needed, and serve.

SERVES 4 TO 6

SQUID, TOMATOES, AND MINT

CALAMARI, POMODORO E MENTA

This sauce can be easily made a few hours ahead. Quickly cook the squid and place on a plate. (Cooking for too long will make the squid tough.) Make the sauce and simmer until medium thick. When the pasta is ready, combine squid and sauce, briefly stir it over a medium heat, and toss with the spaghetti.

½ cup extra virgin olive oil

1 pound clean squid body cut into ½-inch rings

½ cup finely chopped yellow onion

2 cloves garlic, minced

2 tablespoons rinsed, minced capers

4 cups canned Italian plum tomatoes, with juice and put through a food mill to remove seeds

Salt and hot red pepper flakes, to taste

4 to 5 mint leaves, minced

2 tablespoons minced parsley

1 pound spaghetti

1 Heat the oil in a wide-bottom saucepan over medium heat. Add the squid pieces and cook, stirring until they just begin to color, 1 to 2 minutes. With a slotted spoon, transfer squid to a plate and set aside.

2 Add onion to the saucepan and cook, stirring, until lightly golden, 3 to 4 minutes. Add the garlic and capers and stir until garlic begins to color, about 1 minute. Add the tomatoes and season with salt and red pepper flakes. As soon as the sauce begins to simmer, reduce the heat to medium-low and cook, uncovered, stirring occasionally, until sauce has a medium-thick consistency, 5 to 7 minutes.

3 Return the squid to the pan, add the mint and parsley, and simmer 1 to 2 minutes longer. Taste and adjust the seasoning.

4 Meanwhile, cook spaghetti in boiling, salted water according to package directions.

5 Drain pasta and place in a warm serving bowl. Add about half of the sauce and quickly toss to combine. Add a little more sauce, if needed. Serve immediately.

SERVE 4 TO 6

SQUID WITH BROCCOLI RABE

CALAMARI CON BROCCOLI RAPE

The people of southern Italy love broccoli rabe because of its slightly bitter and nutty taste. And when this vegetable is paired with seafood and pasta, for me, it is a marriage made in heaven.

1 bunch broccoli rabe

½ cup extra virgin olive oil

2 cloves garlic, minced

3 anchovy filets, minced

Hot red pepper flakes, to taste

1 pound cleaned squid body, cut into 1-inch rings

1 pound spaghetti

2 slices of Italian bread, toasted and crumbled very fine in a food processor

1 Trim and discard any large woody stalks and wilted leaves from the broccoli. Peel the thinner stems, wash the broccoli well under cold running water, and cut into smaller pieces.

2 Bring a large pot of salted water to a boil. Add the broccoli and stems and cook until very tender, 5 to 6 minutes. Drain and plunge the broccoli into a bowl of iced water to cool. Drain again, pat dry with paper towels, and roughly chop. Set aside.

3 Heat the oil in a large skillet over medium heat. Add the garlic, anchovies, red pepper flakes, and the squid rings. Stir, just long enough to barely color the squid, about 1 minute. Add the broccoli and stir just long enough to heat through.

4 Meanwhile, cook spaghetti in boiling salted water according to package directions.

5 Drain pasta, place it in the skillet with the squid, and stir a few times. Serve with a little sprinkle of crisp bread crumbs.

SERVES 4 TO 6

RAGU

108 Bologna White Meat Ragu

110 Lamb and Bell Pepper Ragu

112 Meat Ragu Bologna Style

114 Meat Ragu Neapolitan Style

115 Rabbit, Tomato, and Olive Ragu

116 Meat Ragu and Porcini Mushrooms

118 Sausage, Fava Beans, Tomato, and Cream Ragu

119 Sausage and Lamb Ragu

120 Veal Shank Ragu with Fresh Tomatoes and Peas

123 Sausage, Prosciutto, Onion, and Saffron-Cream Ragu

BOLOGNA WHITE MEAT RAGU
RAGU DI CARNE BIANCHE DI BOLOGNA

Make sure to cook this and any other ragu in this chapter in a wide-bottom saucepan. The wide pan will evaporate the juices of the meat very quickly so the meat will begin to brown, thus giving more flavor to the sauce.

4 tablespoons unsalted butter

1 cup finely minced shallots

1 pound ground veal

½ pound ground chicken breasts

2 ounces pancetta, minced

1 cup dry white wine

1 to 2 cups chicken broth, divided

3 cups milk

Salt and freshly ground white pepper, to taste

2 tablespoons minced parsley

1 pound spaghetti

1 cup freshly grated Parmigiano-Reggiano cheese

1 Heat the butter in a wide-bottom saucepan. When the butter begins to foam, add the shallots and cook, stirring with a wooden spoon until shallots are soft and lightly colored, 3 to 4 minutes.

2 Raise the heat to high; add the veal, chicken, and pancetta and cook, stirring until the meat is lightly golden, 7 to 8 minutes.

3 Add the wine and stir until wine is almost all reduced. Add 1 cup broth, stir for a few minutes, and then add the milk. Season with salt and white pepper. Reduce the heat to low, cover the pan with the lid slightly askew, and cook, stirring occasionally for 45 to 50 minutes. Stir the parsley into the ragu, taste, and adjust the seasoning. At this point the ragu should have a medium-thick consistency. Add a little more broth, if needed.

4 Meanwhile, cook spaghetti in boiling salted water according to package directions.

5 Drain pasta and place in a warm serving bowl. Add about half of the ragu and quickly toss to combine. Add a little more ragu, if needed. Serve with a sprinkling of Parmigiano.

SERVES 4 TO 6

LAMB AND BELL PEPPER RAGU

RAGU DI AGNELLO E PEPERONI

Southern Italians love lamb and they cook it in myriad ways. Here bell peppers are added to lamb and tomatoes, imparting this ragu with a mellow sweet flavor.

½ cup extra virgin olive oil

3 red bell peppers, seeded and cut into ½-inch pieces

1 cup finely minced yellow onion

1 pound ground lamb shoulder

1 cup dry white wine

3 cups canned Italian plum tomatoes, with juice and put through a food mill to remove seeds

1 cup chicken broth,

Salt and hot red pepper flakes, to taste

1 pound spaghetti

½ cup freshly grated Pecorino Romano cheese

1 Heat the oil in a wide-bottom saucepan over medium heat. Add the bell peppers and onion and stir until onion is lightly golden and soft, about 5 minutes. Raise the heat to high and add the lamb; stir until lamb loses its raw color, 4 to 5 minutes. Add the wine and cook until wine is reduced approximately by half. Add the tomatoes and broth, season with salt and red pepper flakes, and bring to a boil.

2 Reduce the heat to low; partially cover the pan and cook, stirring from time to time, until the sauce has a medium-thick consistency, 1 to1 ½ hours. Taste, adjust the seasoning, and set aside.

3 Meanwhile, cook spaghetti in boiling salted water according to package directions.

4 Drain pasta and place in a warm serving bowl. Add about half of the ragu and quickly toss to combine. Add a little more sauce, if needed. Serve with a sprinkle of Pecorino Romano cheese.

SERVES 4 TO 6

MEAT RAGU BOLOGNA STYLE
RAGU ALLA BOLOGNESE

This is the classic ragu of Bologna, the city where I was born and raised. It is also the ragu that coated the homemade tagliatelle my mother would make on Sundays. This ragu, however, is also terrific over rigatoni, penne, and spaghetti.

1 (28-ounce) can whole peeled Italian tomatoes, preferably San Marzano

5 tablespoons unsalted butter, divided

1/3 cup minced onion

1/3 cup minced carrot

1/3 cup minced celery

2 ounces pancetta, minced

1/2 pound ground veal

1/2 pound ground pork

1/2 pound ground beef

Salt and freshly ground pepper, to taste

1 cup dry red wine

1/2 cup milk

1 pound spaghetti

1 cup freshly grated Parmigiano-Reggiano cheese

1 Purée the tomatoes and their juices through a food mill or in a blender until smooth. Set aside.

2 Place 4 tablespoons of the butter in a wide-bottom saucepan over medium heat. When the butter begins to foam, add the onion, carrot, and celery and stir until vegetables begin to soften, 5 to 6 minutes. Add the pancetta, veal, pork, and beef. Raise the heat to high and stir until the meat has a golden color, 8 to 10 minutes. Season lightly with salt and pepper.

3 Add the wine and cook, stirring until most of it has evaporated, about 4 to 5 minutes. Add the tomatoes and bring to a boil. Reduce the heat to low and simmer, stirring from time to time, until sauce has a medium-thick consistency, 1 1/2 to 2 hours. Add the milk and simmer 10 minutes longer. Taste, adjust the seasoning, and turn off the heat.

4 Cook spaghetti in boiling salted water according to package directions.

5 Drain pasta and place in a large warm serving bowl. Add the remaining butter, half of the ragu, and a small handful of the Parmigiano and quickly toss to combine. Serve at once with more sauce, if needed, and a little more cheese.

SERVES 4 TO 6

MEAT RAGU NEAPOLITAN STYLE

SUGO DI CARNE ALLA NAPOLETANA

My mother-in-law used to make this ragu by gently cooking the meat in tomatoes for several hours. The sauce, which was thick and delicious, was tossed with the pasta, and the meat was served as a second course.

½ cup extra virgin olive oil

2½ to 3 pounds Boston butt

Salt and freshly ground pepper, to taste

1 large onion, diced

2 cloves garlic, minced

3 to 4 oil-packed anchovies, minced

⅓ cup chopped flat-leaf parsley

1 cup dry white wine

⅓ cup tomato paste

4 cups canned Italian plum tomatoes, with juice and put through a food mill to remove seeds

1 cup chicken broth

½ cup of freshly grated Pecorino Romano or Parmigiano-Reggiano cheese

1 Preheat the oven to 350 F. Heat the oil in a large wide-bottom oven-proof saucepan over medium heat. Season the pork with salt and a generous amount of pepper, add to the pan, and cook until the pork has a golden color on all sides, 8 to 10 minutes. Transfer meat to a platter.

2 Discard some of the fat in the saucepan and add the onion. Cook, stirring until onion has a nice golden color, 5 to 6 minutes. Add the garlic, anchovies, and parsley and stir for 1 to 2 minutes. Raise the heat to high, add the wine and stir until wine is reduce by half. Add the tomato paste and quickly stir until it is well incorporated into the wine, 1 to 2 minutes. Add the tomatoes and stir until mixture begin to simmer. Turn off the heat.

3 Return the meat to the saucepan, cover the top with aluminum foil, and place on the middle rack of the oven. Simmer, stirring every half hour or so, for about 2 to 2 ½ hours or until the meat begins to flake off when it is pierced with a fork. Turn the meat a few times during cooking. Add a little chicken broth if sauce reduces too much.

4 Remove the meat from the pan and place on a cutting board, cover loosely with foil. Meanwhile, cook spaghetti in boiling salted water according to package directions.

5 Drain the pasta and place in a large serving bowl. Add a few ladles of the tomato sauce and a nice handful of cheese and toss to combine. Taste, adjust the seasoning, and serve. Slice meat and serve separately.

VARIATION: If you do not want to serve the meat as a second course, chop it into very small pieces, stir it into the sauce, and serve.

SERVES 4 TO 6

RABBIT, TOMATO, AND OLIVE RAGU

CONIGLIO CON POMODORO, OLIVE E SALVIA

I love the mild flavor, firm texture, and versatility of rabbit.

½ cup extra virgin olive oil, divided

1 rabbit, about 1½ to 2 pounds, cut into pieces

Flour

1 cup finely minced yellow onion

8 to 10 black olives, minced

2 cloves garlic, minced

1 cup dry Marsala wine, such as Florio or Pellegrino

3 cups canned Italian plum tomatoes, with juice and put through a food mill to remove seeds

2 cups chicken broth, divided

Salt and freshly ground pepper,

1 pound spaghetti

½ cup freshly grated Parmigiano-Reggiano cheese

1 Heat half of the oil in a wide-bottom skillet over high heat. Lightly flour the rabbit pieces and add to the hot skillet without crowding. Cook, turning once, until golden on both sides, 8 to 10 minutes. Transfer to a platter.

2 Discard the oil and place the skillet back over medium heat. Add the remaining oil, and when it is hot, add the onion. Cook, stirring until onion is golden and soft, 6 to 8 minutes. Add the olives and garlic and stir for a minute or two.

3 Raise the heat to high, pour in the wine and bring to a boil. Stir, scraping up any browned bits from the bottom of the pan, and cook until wine is reduced by half. Add the tomatoes and 1 cup of the broth, season with salt and pepper, and bring to a gentle boil.

4 Return the rabbit pieces to the pan and stir into the sauce, cover the pan, and cook, over medium-low heat, stirring from time to time and turning the pieces until rabbit is tender and the sauce has a medium-thick consistency, 45 to 50 minutes. Turn off the heat.

5 When cool enough to handle, transfer the rabbit to a cutting board. Remove the meat from the bones, discard the bones, and chop the meat very fine. Return the meat to the sauce and stir, over low heat until the meat is well blended with the sauce, 4 to 5 minutes. Taste and adjust the seasoning. If sauce is too thick, add a little more broth.

6 Meanwhile, cook spaghetti in boiling salted water according to package directions.

7 Drain pasta and place in a warm serving bowl. Add about half of the sauce and quickly toss to combine. Add a little more sauce, if needed. Serve with a sprinkling of Parmigiano cheese.

SERVES 4 TO 6

MEAT RAGU AND PORCINI MUSHROOMS

RAGU' DI CARNE E PORCINI

Every time I make a ragu, I double the amount of the ingredients. I use what I need and freeze the leftovers for another time.

1 ounce dried porcini mushrooms, soaked in 2 cups lukewarm water for 20 minutes

4 tablespoons unsalted butter

1 cup finely minced yellow onion

¾ pound ground veal

¾ pound ground pork

1 cup dry white wine

3 cups canned Italian plum tomatoes, with juice and put through a food mill to remove seeds

½ cup milk

Salt and pepper, to taste

1 cup chicken broth or water

1 pound spaghetti

½ cup freshly grated Parmigiano-Reggiano cheese

1 Drain the mushrooms and reserve the soaking water. Rinse the mushrooms well under cold running water and mince. Line a strainer with paper towels and strain the reserved liquid into a bowl to remove the sandy deposit. Set aside.

2 Heat the butter in a wide-bottom saucepan over medium heat. When the butter begins to foam, add the onion and cook, stirring, until pale yellow and soft, 4 to 5 minutes. Raise the heat to high, add the veal and pork, and stir with a wooden spoon until the meat begins to color, 4 to 5 minutes. Add the wine and keep stirring until wine is almost all reduced. Add the mushrooms and cook just long enough to combine. Add 1 cup of the reserved porcini soaking water, the tomatoes, and milk and season with salt and pepper.

3 Reduce the heat to low, cover the pan leaving the lid slightly askew, and cook, stirring from time to time, 45 minutes to 1 hour. Taste and adjust the seasoning. If sauce seems too thick, add some chicken broth or water.

4 Meanwhile, cook spaghetti in boiling salted water according to package directions.

5 Drain pasta and place in a warm serving bowl. Add about half of the ragu and quickly toss to combine. Add a little more sauce, if needed. Serve with a sprinkling of Parmigiano.

SERVES 4 TO 6

SAUSAGE, FAVA BEANS, TOMATO, AND CREAM RAGU

SALSICCIA, FAVE, POMODORO E PANNA

There is always a meat ragu at my restaurant in Sacramento—hardier and richly golden in fall and winter and lighter in spring and summer, just like this ragu. This ragu is one of my favorites, and it pairs very well with spaghetti but also with rigatoni and penne.

⅓ cup extra virgin olive oil

4 tablespoons unsalted butter, divided

1 cup yellow onion, finely minced

1 cup carrot, minced

1 pound mild Italian sausage, skinned and finely chopped

1 cup dry white wine

1 cup low sodium chicken broth

4 cups canned Italian plum tomatoes, with juice and put through a food mill to remove seeds

½ cup heavy cream

1½ cups shelled fava beans, blanched, or frozen peas, thawed

Salt, to taste

1 pound spaghetti

½ cup freshly grated Parmigiano-Reggiano cheese

1 Heat the oil and 2 tablespoons butter in a wide-bottom heavy saucepan over medium heat. Add the onion and carrot and stir until the onion is pale yellow and soft, 5 to 6 minutes. Add the sausage, breaking up into small pieces, and stir until it is lightly golden.

2 Add the wine. When wine is almost all reduced, add the broth and tomatoes. As soon as the liquid comes to a boil, reduce the heat to low and cook, stirring from time to time, until ragu has a medium-thick consistency, 45 minutes to 1 hour. Add the cream and fava beans, season with salt, and simmer 10 minutes longer. Taste, adjust the seasoning, and turn off the heat.

3 Meanwhile, cook spaghetti in boiling salted water according to package directions.

4 Drain pasta and place in a warm serving bowl. Add about half of the sauce, the remaining butter, and a small handful of Parmigiano. Quickly toss until pasta and sauce are well combined. Taste and adjust the seasoning and serve.

SERVES 4 TO 6

SAUSAGE AND LAMB RAGU

SUGO DI SALSICCIA E AGNELLO ALLA SARDA

Meat ragu is one of the most loved dishes that consistently appears on the menus of the trattorie of Italy. The ragu is different from area to area, but the long, slow cooking process is the same.

⅓ cup extra virgin olive oil

2 tablespoons unsalted butter

1 cup minced leeks, white part only

2 tablespoons chopped Italian parsley

2 cloves garlic, minced

½ pound sweet Italian sausage, skinned and chopped into small pieces

1 pound chopped lamb, preferably from the shoulder

1 cup dry white wine

4 cups canned Italian plum tomatoes, with juice and put through a food mill to remove seeds

Salt and freshly ground pepper, to taste

1 cup chicken broth

1 pound spaghetti

1 cup freshly grated Pecorino Romano or Parmigiano-Reggiano cheese

1 Heat the oil and butter in a wide-bottom saucepan over medium heat. When the oil is hot, but not smoking, add the leeks and cook, stirring until they are lightly golden and soft, 4 to 5 minutes. Add the parsley and garlic and stir until it just begins to color. Add the sausage and lamb and stir, breaking the meat down with a wooden spoon, until it has a light golden color, 7 to 8 minutes. Add the wine and stir until liquid is reduced approximately by half.

2 Add the tomatoes, bring to a boil, and lightly season with salt and pepper. Reduce the heat to low, cover the pan with the lid slightly askew, and cook, stirring from time to time, for about 1 hour. At the end of cooking, the sauce should be moist with a medium-thick consistency. If too thick, stir in the broth. Taste and adjust the seasoning.

3 Meanwhile, cook spaghetti in boiling salted water according to package direction.

4 Drain the pasta and place in a large serving bowl. Add a few ladles of the meat sauce and a nice handful of the cheese and toss to combine. Taste, adjust the seasoning, and serve with a little more ragu or cheese if needed.

SERVES 4 TO 6

VEAL SHANK RAGU WITH FRESH TOMATOES AND PEAS

RAGU DI OSSOBUCO DI VITELLO CON PISELLI

Every time I make this dish for my family, I always double the recipe. One day I serve it as it was intended, with the meat whole and the sauce on top. Then the next day, I mince the leftover meat, put it back into the sauce, and serve it with spaghetti or another pasta.

3 veal shanks, cut into 1½-inch thick slices

Salt and freshly ground pepper, to taste

½ cup flour

½ cup extra virgin olive oil

2 tablespoons unsalted butter

1 cup minced onion

½ cup minced carrots

½ cup minced celery

1 cup dry white wine

2 cups chicken broth

2 pounds fresh tomatoes, seeded and diced

1 cup shelled peas, blanched, or frozen peas, thawed

1 pound spaghetti

½ cup freshly grated Parmigiano-Reggiano cheese

1 Heat the oven to 325 F.

2 Sprinkle the veal with salt and pepper, dredge in flour, and shake off any excess.

3 Heat the oil in a wide-bottom oven-proof saucepan over medium heat. When the oil is hot, add the veal and brown on all sides, 8 to 10 minutes. Transfer veal to a dish. Discard some of the oil in the pan, if needed.

4 Add the butter to the pan and when it begins to foam, add onion, carrots, and celery and cook, stirring occasionally, until vegetables are tender, about 10 minutes.

5 Return the veal to the pan, raise the heat to high and add the wine. Stir, scraping the bottom of the pan with a wooden spoon, until wine is reduced by half. Stir in the broth and tomatoes and bring to a boil. Turn off the heat, partially cover the pan with a lid, and put in the center of the oven. Cook, turning the meat every half hour or so until it is fork tender and begins to fall apart when pierced with a fork, about 1 ½ hours.

6 When cool enough to handle, transfer the veal to a cutting board.

continued on page 122

Remove the meat from the bones and mince into small pieces. Return the meat to the sauce, add the peas and stir well over medium-low heat to incorporate, 3 to 4 minutes. Taste and adjust the seasoning.

7 Meanwhile, cook spaghetti in boiling salted water according to package instructions.

8 Drain pasta and place in a warm serving bowl. Add about half of the ragu and quickly toss to combine. Add a little more sauce, if needed. Serve with a sprinkling of Parmigiano-Reggiano cheese.

SERVES 4 TO 6

SAUSAGE, PROSCIUTTO, ONION, AND SAFFRON-CREAM RAGU

RAGU DI SALSICCIA, PROSCIUTTO, CIPOLLE, PANNA E ZAFFERANO

One of the most sought after dishes on the menus of the trattorie in the Emilia-Romagna region, are the ones with sausage ragu. These ragus often include other types of meats, prosciutto, onions, wine, broth, tomatoes, or cream and are quick to prepare and deliciously decadent.

2 teaspoons saffron threads

¼ cup water

4 tablespoons unsalted butter

1½ cups minced onion

1 clove garlic, minced

¾ pound sweet Italian sausage, skin removed and finely chopped

¼ pound sliced prosciutto, finely diced

1 cup dry white wine

1½ cups heavy cream

Salt, to taste

1 cup chicken broth

1 pound spaghetti

1 cup freshly grated Parmigiano-Reggiano cheese

1 Soak the saffron threads in water for 15 to 20 minutes. Set aside.

2 Heat the butter in a wide-bottom saucepan over medium heat. Add the onion and cook until onion has a light golden color, 5 to 6 minutes. Add the garlic, stir once or twice, and then add the sausage. Stir, breaking the meat down with a wooden spoon until sausage has lost its raw color, 6 to 7 minutes. Add the prosciutto and wine and stir until wine is almost all evaporated, 1 to 2 minutes. Add the saffron water, stir for about 1 minute, and then add the cream. Season with salt and stir until sauce has a medium-thick consistency, 2 to 3 minutes. Add a little more broth if sauce is too thick.

3 Meanwhile, cook spaghetti in boiling salted water according to package directions.

4 Drain pasta and place in a warm serving bowl. Add about half of the ragu and quickly toss to combine. Add a little more ragu, if needed. Serve with a sprinkling of Parmigiano.

SERVED 4 TO 6

ACKNOWLEDGMENTS

This book would not have happened if my six grandchildren had not insisted that each dinner I prepared for them was the much loved spaghetti—spaghetti with simple sauces that could be put together in the time the pasta was cooking and made with fresh, savory, and easy-to-find ingredients.

With this cookbook I have tried to keep the sauces quite simple so that when my grandchildren leave for college these recipes will guide them and, in each bite, they will recapture the flavor of home.

I also want to acknowledge the following people whose work enriched my book:

Su Her, the best sous chef I have ever had. His great palate, energy, and intuition made this project so much easier;

The talented Jessica Nicosia-Nadler, whose photographs are simply mouthwatering and enrich the book;

Karen Hand, for going over the manuscript and for keeping my schedule straight. You are the best!

METRIC CONVERSION CHART

Volume Measurements		Weight Measurements		Temperature Conversion	
U.S.	Metric	U.S.	Metric	Fahrenheit	Celsius
1 teaspoon	5 ml	1/2 ounce	15 g	250	120
1 tablespoon	15 ml	1 ounce	30 g	300	150
1/4 cup	60 ml	3 ounces	90 g	325	160
1/3 cup	75 ml	4 ounces	115 g	350	180
1/2 cup	125 ml	8 ounces	225 g	375	190
2/3 cup	150 ml	12 ounces	350 g	400	200
3/4 cup	175 ml	1 pound	450 g	425	220
1 cup	250 ml	2 1/4 pounds	1 kg	450	230

INDEX

A

Alcohol
    Marsala Wine: 115
    Red Wine: 112
    Vodka: 59, 99
    White Wine: 90, 95, 100, 108, 110, 114, 116, 118, 119, 120, 123
Anchovies: 26, 44, 54, 62, 64, 73, 88, 95, 102, 104, 114
Artichoke: 68
Arugula: 37, 44, 48
Asparagus: 43, 69

B

Balsamic Vinegar: 50, 76, 81

Basil: 12, 15, 26, 32, 36, 37, 38, 42, 49, 52, 53, 54, 81, 92
Beef, ground: 112
Bell Pepper: 76, 81, 110
Boston Butt: 114
Bottarga: 89
Broccoli: 34, 70, 97
Broccoli Rabe: 104
Butternut Squash: 71

C

Capers: 23, 44, 50, 62, 68, 72, 73, 94, 102, 103
Carrot: 49, 112, 118, 120
Cauliflower: 72
Celery: 49, 52, 112, 120

Cheese
    Goat: 11, 12, 42, 53,
    Gorgonzola: 28
    Mascarpone: 16
    Mozzarella: 15, 26, 50
    Pecorino Romano: 14, 17, 21, 24, 32, 40, 48, 54, 56, 64, 110, 114, 119
    Ricotta: 11, 12, 37, 53
    Smoked Mozzarella: 23
    Swiss: 20
    Taleggio: 25
Chicken: 108
Clams: 90
Cream: 10, 20, 25, 28, 37, 58, 59, 71, 74, 99, 100, 118, 123

E

Egg: 16, 18, 69
Eggplant: 73, 81, 94

F

Fava Beans: 69, 80, 118
Fish and Seafood
    Anchovies: 26, 44, 54, 62, 64, 73,
        88, 95, 102, 104, 114
    Bottarga: 89
    Clams: 90
    Lobster: 92
    Monkfish: 95
    Mussels: 96
    Prawns: 97
    Salmon: 100
    Scallops: 98

    Shrimp: 99
    Squid: 103, 104
    Swordfish: 94
    Tuna: 102

G

Goat Cheese: 11, 12, 42, 53
Gorgonzola: 28

H

Ham, smoked: 69
Herbs and Spices
    Basil: 12, 15, 26, 32, 36, 37, 38,
        42, 49, 52, 53, 54, 81, 92
    Mint: 103
    Nutmeg: 10
    Oregano: 26, 54, 56, 60, 75

    Parsley: 24, 51, 58, 82, 114
    Saffron: 24, 96, 123
    Sage: 11, 22, 82

L

Lamb: 110, 119
Leeks: 119
Lobster: 92

M

Marsala Wine: 115
Mascarpone: 16
Meat
    Beef, ground: 112
    Lamb: 110, 119
    Rabbit: 115
    Sausage, Italian: 70, 118, 119,
        123
    Veal
        ground: 108, 112, 116
        shank: 120
Mint: 103
Monkfish: 95
Mozzarella: 15, 26, 50
Mushrooms: 74, 82
    Porcini: 116
Mussels: 96

N

Nutmeg: 10
Nuts
    Pine Nuts: 32, 38, 42, 88
    Walnuts: 28, 36, 37

O

Olives
    Black: 38, 44, 62, 64, 68, 72, 94,
        95, 102, 115
    Green: 23, 62

Onion: 17, 49, 52, 60, 76, 84, 94, 97, 103, 110, 112, 114, 115, 116, 118, 120, 123

Oregano: 26, 54, 56, 60, 75

P

Pancetta: 16, 17, 18, 24, 59, 60, 84, 108, 112

Parsley: 24, 51, 58, 82, 114

Peas: 18, 43, 69, 78, 120

Pecorino Romano: 14, 17, 21, 24, 32, 40, 48, 54, 56, 64, 110, 114, 119

Porcini Mushrooms: 116

Pork,
    Boston Butt: 114
    ground: 112, 116
    Ham, smoked: 69
    Pancetta: 16, 17, 18, 24, 59, 60, 84, 108, 112
    Prosciutto: 20, 22, 51, 74, 78, 123

Potato, Yukon Gold: 45

Poultry, see Chicken

Prawns: 97

Prosciutto: 20, 22, 51, 74, 78, 123

R

Rabbit: 115

Raisins: 88

Red Wine: 112

Ricotta: 11, 12, 37, 53

S

Saffron: 24, 96, 123

Sage: 11, 22, 82

Salmon: 100

Sausage, Italian: 70, 118, 119, 123

Scallops: 98

Seafood, see Fish

Shallots: 64, 71, 78, 80, 96, 100, 108

Shrimp: 99

Smoked Mozzarella: 23

Squid: 103, 104

Swiss Cheese: 20

Swordfish: 94

T

Taleggio Cheese: 25

Tomatoes:
    Cherry: 15, 38, 50, 80, 96, 98
    Fresh: 12, 26, 40, 49, 52, 53, 56, 76, 92, 120
    Plum: 14, 48, 51, 54, 58, 59, 60, 61, 62, 64, 78, 95, 99, 102, 103, 110, 112, 114, 115, 116, 118, 119
    Sun-dried: 14, 23, 36, 44, 51, 89, 92, 94

Tuna: 102

V

Veal
    ground: 108, 112, 116
    shank: 120

Vegetables
    Artichoke: 68
    Arugula: 37, 44, 48,
    Asparagus: 43, 69
    Bell Pepper: 76, 81, 110
    Broccoli: 34, 70, 97
    Broccoli Rabe: 104
    Butternut Squash: 71
    Carrot: 49, 112, 118, 120
    Cauliflower: 72
    Celery: 49, 52, 112, 120
    Eggplant: 73, 81, 94
    Fava Beans: 69, 80, 118

Leeks: 119

Mushrooms: 74, 82
    Porcini: 116

Onion: 17, 49, 52, 60, 76, 84, 94, 97, 103, 110, 112, 114, 115, 116, 118, 120, 123

Peas: 18, 43, 69, 78, 120

Potato, Yukon Gold: 45

Shallots: 64, 71, 78, 80, 96, 100, 108

Tomatoes:
    Cherry: 15, 38, 50, 80, 96, 98
    Fresh: 12, 26, 40, 49, 52, 53, 56, 76, 92, 120
    Plum: 14, 48, 51, 54, 58, 59, 60, 61, 62, 64, 78, 95, 99, 102, 103, 110, 112, 114, 115, 116, 118, 119
    Sun-dried: 14, 23, 36, 44, 51, 89, 92, 94

Zucchini: 81, 84

Vodka: 59, 99

W

White Wine: 90, 95, 100, 108, 110, 114, 116, 118, 119, 120, 123

Z

Zucchini: 81, 84

Biba Caggiano is the chef/owner of BIBA Restaurant in Sacramento, California. Biba is also the award-winning author of eight best-selling cookbooks and is still recognized for her previous internationally syndicated cooking show *Biba's Italian Kitchen* on the Learning Channel. Her restaurant is the recipient of many glowing awards and recognitions from the Governor of California, the Senate of the State of California, the California Legislature Assembly, Food Network Canada, and many trade publications such as *Wine Spectator, Conde' Nast Travelers, Gourmet Magazine, Travel and Leisure, Taste of Italia*, and *Fine Cooking Magazine*. When not spending time with her family, she can be found daily in her restaurant.